CAFE

CAFE BEAUJOLAIS

Margaret S. Fox
and
John Bear

Ten Speed Press

Dedication

To my grandparents, whose spirit of adventure has profoundly influenced me.

TEN SPEED PRESS
Post Office Box 7123
Berkeley, California 94707

You may order single copies prepaid direct from the publisher for $9.95 plus $.85 postage and handling (California residents add 6% state sales tax; Bay Area residents add 6½%).

Library of Congress Catalog Number: 84-051172

ISBN: 0-89815-134-1

Book design and production by Fifth Street Design, Berkeley

The recipes and notes for Peppery Shrimp Dumpling Soup with Chinese Greens and Roasted Szechwan Pepper-Salt on pages 130 and 131 are copyright © 1984 by Barbara Tropp. The recipe for Boeuf à l'Orange Indienne on page 156 is copyright © 1984 by Jay Perkins.

Illustrations by Pedro Gonzalez

Photography provided by and copyright © 1984 by: Nicholas Wilson, John Bear, Brenton Beck, J. Clifton Meek, D. Podden, and Anne Fox.

Printed in the United States of America

9 10 11 12 — 93 92 91 90

Table of Contents

Recipes

Recipe Index

Desserts

Acknowledgements

Some authors write short acknowledgements; others make them an extra chapter. I belong to the latter group, because so many special people have contributed to making Cafe Beaujolais a viable and enjoyable business over these seven and a half years.

Thanks to:

My family, Harold, Anne, and Emily Fox, for their worrying, infinite understanding and caring, financial and emotional support, and everpresent sense of humor during both difficult and wonderful times; My grandmother, Ida Kravitz, who thinks I can do *anything*, and whose business acumen continually amazes me; Patricia Priano, the restaurant's manager and a fellow lefthander, for her business sense, focus, honesty and sensitivity, which have guided Cafe Beaujolais into the real world; Gary Jenanyan, for his generously shared business expertise and dependable friendship; Hilde, David and Stephen Burton, for their confidence in me over the years, and for their appreciation of fine food; Stephanie Kroninger, a brilliant graphic artist, who designed our bird logo; Christine Hock, our bookkeeper, for her loyalty, accuracy, and frankness; Barbara Tropp, for her yearly Chinese feasts at Cafe Beaujolais, and for her caring friendship; Miriam Connolly, for her lifesaving assistance; Sally Jean Shepard, for her high standards, readiness to laugh, and sincere belief in thank you letters; The Amberger-Kroninger family, who cheerfully ate successful and not-so-successful culinary experiments; Mary Ellen Black for being a great friend; Lorraine Jaggli, for her unique blend of wackiness and seriousness, and for her belief in the work ethic; Michael Thorburn, for his *savoir-faire* and his help at an important time; Desiree Douglass and Josh Shook, for creating a most beautiful garden and a haven for hummingbirds; Blossom Elfman, whose inspirational scrambled eggs may have been the beginning of all of this; Clay Wollard, talented pastry chef, for the world's best haircuts; Judy Carrell, for her dedication and cheerfulness; Paul Carrell, for never being too busy to rescue us from the latest disaster; John Wetzler (plumber) and Jim Czadek (electrician) for their continued attentiveness during our many crises; The Cafe Beaujolais staff, a remarkable group of hard workers who know how to have a good time; All the wonderful customers who so enthusiastically support Cafe Beaujolais; All the recipe testers, whose patience in testing and retesting amazed me: Susannah Bear, Anne Fox, Jeffery Garcia, Daniel Helsel, B Kruse, Karen Sprague, Kathryn Wentzel (who travelled from Amsterdam to perform this noble deed), and Jose Manuel Yanez; All the recipe contributors for sharing their delicious creations; Tim Savinar and Larry Richardson, for their sensitive and responsible professionalism; Erich Schmid and the Savings Bank of Mendocino County, for their extraordinary belief in my business, despite the odds; Phil Wood and George Young of Ten Speed Press for making this all possible, and Jackie Wan and Marina Bear for their editing excellence.

And to John Bear for his encouragement of, and participation in this project, and for his finely developed sense of the absurd.

INTRODUCTION

Seven Things to Know About This Book

1. Why This Is Not (Just) a Cook Book

Of the 256 pages in this book, 132 are devoted to specific recipes and how to prepare them, and 124 are not. That, in part, is why it says "Cafe Beaujolais" on the cover and not "Cafe Beaujolais Cookbook."

It is a book about Cafe Beaujolais, and so it includes, of course, recipes for most of the dishes that made the restaurant famous (to the extent it is). But it is also a book about food and about the restaurant business, and how to start one (and why maybe you shouldn't); and it is about Margaret Fox, the woman who owns, runs, and cooks at Cafe Beaujolais.

This is why the book is neither comprehensive in its culinary scope (as per *Joy of Cooking* or *Betty Crocker's Cookbook*); nor definitive in its gimmickry (42,000 recipes for pasta, or chocolate, or casseroles, or chocolate pasta casseroles, or whatever). If there is disproportionate emphasis on desserts and on breakfast-related items, that is simply because that is the way things are at the restaurant, and for its owner.

2. Where the Book Came From

"I've calculated that I've had just about 100,000 meals in my life, and that was one of the very best. Those two young ladies were just dears. Charming and oh, so efficient. Put that in your book."
—Ninety-two-year-old Customer

John Bear, who writes books of all kinds for Ten Speed Press, was taken to lunch at Chez Panisse in Berkeley by the two gentlemen who operate that publishing house. The *Chez Panisse Menu Cookbook* had recently been published by Random House, The notion arose that there might be a place in the world for another book by a prominent woman owner/chef—but this one a book about food, and styles of cooking, and operating a restaurant, as well as a book of recipes and cooking information and anecdotes and stories.

John Bear mentioned the fact that California's *other* well-known woman-chef-owned restaurant happened to be located in the very village in which he lived; that its proprietor, Margaret Fox, was articulate, witty, and not exactly publicity-shy; and that although Ten Speed already had a dozen splendid and successful cookbooks on its list, it really had no books *about* cooking.

Thus a bargain was struck, and the result is in your hands.

This really is Margaret Fox's book. John Bear helped out enough with the text and the recipe introductions to get his name on the title page—but whenever the first person singular is used, the "I" is Margaret's.

3. **What Has Been Left Out, and Why**

All of our popular dishes have been included in this book, with two significant exceptions. So if you bought the book to learn the secret of Chocolate Sin, or the Beaujolais Waffles, you're out of luck, and you may as well take it back for a refund now, before you get chocolate stains on page 202, trying some of the other recipes. The reason for leaving those two out is very simple: I am seriously considering marketing Chocolate Sin Cakes, and Beaujolais Waffle Mix to retail stores or by mail order, so I'm not particularly eager to let those secrets out the refrigerator door.

If I decide otherwise, then I promise I'll put the recipes in *Cafe Beaujolais II*. But everything else people keep asking me about is in here. There just aren't that many secrets in the restaurant world anyway. It induces unhealthy paranoia to think that you've got something so secret you must protect it at all costs. Didn't Colonel Sanders lie awake nights worrying about the safekeeping of the formula for his eleven herbs and spices?

So I have no real fear that people all over Northern California will start making my Chicken Stuffed Under the Skin (see page 150) or Chocolate Amazon Cake (page 210) and never come into the restaurant again. If people were so committed to the notion of cooking from cookbooks to the exclusion of eating out, restaurants would have been doomed to oblivion years and years ago.

Another important factor is that we have gained so much over the years from the generosity of others—people who have shared freely of their time and talents, and I simply want to keep on in that vein.

4. Where the Recipes Came From

Culinary philosophers, or perhaps philosophical cooks can argue from now till dinner time (and often do) as to whether there can be such a thing as an original recipe any more. With tens of thousands of cookbooks published in this country alone, the probability that there could be something completely new under the sun may be quite low.

Lawsuits have been fought (and occasionally won) over the matter of whether or not Person A stole or misappropriated a recipe from Person B's restaurant or cookbook.

That doesn't sound like fun. I honestly think of the recipes in this book (with a few exceptions I'll discuss in a moment) as mine. Many of them I have cooked and served to my family, friends, and/or the public for years. Some, to be sure, are modifications of things I have eaten or read about elsewhere. If I see a published recipe calling for maple syrup and raisins and I think to myself, I bet that would be even better with ginger and walnuts, and it is, then the modified recipe is mine. If someone in Indiana has been making exactly the same thing in the same way for fifty-seven years, then more power to them. If it has appeared in their copyrighted cookbook, then I apologize, assure them that I developed my recipe independently, and that a correction will be made in the next edition.

Some of the recipes in the book have come from friends and relatives. In most cases, I invited them to share with the world a particular favorite of mine. For instance, I've been enjoying Gary Jenanyan's mother's rice pilaf for years, and I'm delighted that now you can, too. (See page 168.)

Everything in the book has, however, been cooked and eaten by me—and served in the restaurant, sometimes as a short-run special, and some as part of our virtually permanent and perennial list of favorites.

5. The Problem of Scaling Down Recipes

It wasn't all that easy. There have been times when I thought, "But I've never made only two of anything in my life!" It is clear, nonetheless, that recipes for fifty omelettes or tomato bisque for forty will have limited usefulness.

As many cooks have learned the hard way, reducing or enlarging a recipe is often much more complex than halving or doubling all the ingredients. You might find you need, for example, twice as many eggs, but only 50% more shortening and no extra salt at all.

It took a good deal of trial and error to render all of my recipes into manageable sizes for families of fewer than forty-eight people. But they all work. They've all been thoroughly tested, and although I must apologize for some rather odd measurements (1⅓ cups of this, 9 tablespoons of that), I can assure you that if you follow the instructions (barring horrendous typographical or other errors), you will come out with a product identical to that which we are serving to the public in Mendocino.

6. The Problem of Hard-to-Find Ingredients

It is incredibly annoying to find a terrific-sounding recipe whose key ingredient turns out to be a rare herb that is harvested once every nine years in the rain forests of Indonesia. Or the flank of the Peruvian tree-dwelling camel. Or other commodities not readily available at your local supermarket.

And yet there *are* situations where something obscure or hard to find is utterly essential if the end product is going to come out exactly like ours. The necessary compromise, then, is to list the ingredients I think are best, and then to offer (in most cases) two alternatives: (1) other ingredients (e.g., oregano instead of the blend called "Beaujolais Blend Herbs"); and (2) information on how to order the ingredient by mail. See page 256 for details.

The one exception to all this is Chicken-Apple Sausages. While my recipe (see page 200) will work nicely with other sausages, it just isn't the same. And I am aware of no way at this time to get them other than at the little factory in Yountville, California. (I say "at this time" in the hope that some sausage-by-mail entrepreneur will read these words and figure out how to add that product to his or her line.)

7. Feedback

If you have comments, questions, or complaints, please don't hesitate to write. I much prefer letters to telephone calls, because it is hard to remain civil, helpful, and sane on the phone while dealing with four or five omelette pans, a management crisis, and a dry well. The address is:

Margaret Fox
Cafe Beaujolais
P. O. Box 1236-B
Mendocino, CA 95460.

Thank you.

THE RESTAURANT

About Mendocino

Like the Taj Mahal by moonlight, falling in love, and the experience of childbirth, Mendocino is one of those things in this world that, if you haven't been there, no words, however eloquent, can really explain—and if you have been there, no words are necessary because you already know.

The facts are simple. Mendocino is an unincorporated village of just over 1,000 souls, located on a point of land jutting out into the Pacific Ocean, about 150 miles north of San Francisco.

The Pomo Indians were here first, and lived in the region for centuries. Some still do. The whaling ships came during the second half of the 19th century. The captains built the homes and churches of their New England memories and dreams, which is why, when Hollywood wants a "typical New England town," they often save the travel money and come to Mendocino instead. *East of Eden*, *Summer of '42*, *Johnny Belinda*, *The Russians Are Coming*, *Same Time Next Year*, *Racing with the Moon*, and a passel of horror films (*Cujo*, *Humanoids from the Deep*, *Dead and Buried*) were filmed on our shores.

©1984 Nicholas Wilson

The whalers were followed by the lumberjacks. Huge redwood trees once grew in the area. Some remain in the state parks; most are now 2 by 4's in San Francisco homes.

The third wave of immigration began in the 1950s: city folks discovering the joy of living and working in the country. First came the arts and crafts people who established the now large and thriving Mendocino Art Center. Next came the "flower children," many of whom, individually or in communes, drifted north as the "Haight Ashbury" scene faded away in San Francisco. And finally came (and still come) the young and middle-aged middle-class urban professionals—doctors, lawyers, accountants, teachers, writers, programmers, psychologists, and the like. Many practice another craft once they are here: a high level computer programmer repairs sewing machines; a space scientist runs a plumbing service; a chemical engineer took over a little country market; two nonpracticing physicians operate an antique store; and a woman with a degree in developmental psychology owns and operates a Mendocino restaurant called Cafe Beaujolais.

So here Mendocino sits, a good 3½ hour drive north of the Golden Gate Bridge—half of that on narrow winding roads—near enough so that we are a reasonable destination for a two- or three-day getaway, and yet far enough that we may never suffer the overcommercialized fate of Carmel, Provincetown, and other once-lovely oceanfront communities. Our local airport is fogged in just often enough to make commercial air service impractical. And we still have to drive sixty-five miles over the mountains to reach the nearest McDonald's or Kentucky Fried Chicken.

We locals get into terrible flaps over whether this or that inn can add some more rooms, or the bank can build a new building across the street. But we do so with remarkable amiability because at heart we know that most of our open space is protected forever as state parkland, and the worst that can happen is that we may grow from 2 to 3½ on some urbanization scale of 1 to 100.

We also know that we are all in this together. It's kind of an island mentality. Here we are in this remote isolated

and somewhat fragile locale. One fallen redwood tree can deprive us of our power, our telephones, or even our road to the outside world. Often, politics or lifestyles take a distant backseat in dealing with local matters.

When our ninety-nine-years-in-the-same-local-family weekly newspaper was bought by an out-of-town conglomerate a few years ago, the "What Shall We Do About This" committee included the man from the John Birch Society, the man from the Industrial Workers of the World (alive and well on our coast!), and a bunch of others that a visiting sociologist might have categorized (albeit secretly) as "hippies," "rednecks," and "yuppies" all sitting down for serious reflection and consideration of the importance (or lack of it) of a locally owned press.

I think the fact that Mendocino is a beautiful place is important both to the success of the restaurant, and to my own psychological well-being. Of course the magnificence of the scenery brings in the tourists. Connoisseurs of coastal drives, from Ireland's Dingle Bay to New Zealand's Milford Sound to the road to the Cape of Good Hope, tell me that there is nothing as spectacular as State Highway

1 between San Francisco and Mendocino. On that entire 150-mile drive, you will not see one single fast food franchise outlet, miniature golf course, water slide, wax museum, giant plaster dinosaur, video arcade, or any of the other signs of civilization that have turned the *east* coast's Highway 1 into Plastic City, virtually from Maine to Florida.

I don't flatter myself that legions of people make that long drive from San Francisco *just* for my Herbed Cream Cheese Omelette (see page 182)—so in that sense, it is important that we *are* in a beautiful part of the world that people want to come and inspect.

But for me, it is just as important that I can breathe clean smog-free air, walk down to the headlands to watch the waves crashing against the rocks, and, during spring and fall, see the great whales migrating between their homes in Alaska and Mexico. It is important that when I walk to the post office to collect my mail (no home delivery yet!), I will see (and interact with, if time and energy permit) anywhere from three to thirty people I know. It is important that if (or, rather, when) my well runs dry, I can go to a competitor and borrow water to tide me over, because we're all on this little island of sanity and good will together.

To sum it up, the description of Mendocino that made the most sense to me came from a tourist from the Midwest who said, "You know, this is one of the very few places in the world where the locals and the tourists seem to do the same things for pleasure." Good scenery, good conversation, and good food. What more could you want?

Well, this is not an essay on the sociology, economics, or interpersonal dynamics of Mendocino—but all these factors are, in some way, relevant to the operation of Cafe Beaujolais.

I worked for Jean Troisgros when he was in California as part of a "Great Chefs of France" series. I remember him saying how often people were surprised to discover that some of France's most famous restaurants are local cafes, and not velour-draped caverns with tuxedoed staff surrounding every table. They are, in fact, places where local working people come to eat—that also happen to serve magnificent food, and so the tourists and good food connoisseurs come as well.

That, I think, is what we've achieved at Cafe Beaujolais. It's a local hangout where people come in their work clothes for an omelette or an espresso before work—and it's a place that people will drive for hours to reach because a San Francisco newspaper said we're the best place in the world to come for Sunday brunch.

Both clienteles are essential to our existence.

"If there's a better brunch to be found anywhere, I've never come close. . . .

I could set your mouth watering by mentioning a couple of Sunday specials I had, like waffles with sour cream, wild rice and toasted pecans in the batter, or crêpes stuffed with fresh salmon, asparagus and toasted pecans in Bearnaise sauce.

Wonderful and innovative. But the genius of Margaret Fox is that the simplest breakfast dish comes out tasting like nothing you've ever experienced before."

—Stan Sesser, Restaurant Critic San Francisco Chronicle

What Kind of Restaurant Are We? and Why Do We Get a Book of Our Own?

In its earliest stages, this book was going to be called something like *California Country Cooking*. But as we thought about it, and worked at it, it became clearer and clearer that even if there *is* something called California country cooking out there as an identifiable cuisine (which is very much in doubt), we're not it.

We're undeniably in the country, and we definitely cook, but in reality, we're doing a type of cooking that could just as easily be done in the city. In any city. There's virtually nothing we do that is unique to the country. The tomatoes may be grown a little closer to the restaurant than Four Seasons' tomatoes or Galatoire's tomatoes, and we may be on friendlier terms with the gardener who grew them— but that's part of the mystique, as much as it's part of the cuisine. It isn't as if we milk our own cows and that somehow the milk is so special a city dairy couldn't duplicate it.

What makes us different? I like to think it is a blend of "satisfyingness", care, breakfast, choices, and magic. A few words on each, if I may.

Satisfyingness

"Coming here is such a wonderful experience. The lighting. The colors. You have an elegant meal, and yet it's not stuffy. It's calm and relaxed. It's always there. It's always reliable."
—Regular Customer

We follow no style or school of cooking. We are not an Italian or a French or a Mexican or a Chinese restaurant, although we've served dishes from all these cuisines. We are not a new age or a cosmic cookery or a health food or a nouvelle cuisine establishment, although some of our customers may see us as one of these.

I think basically the only unifying theme is that of being immensely satisfying. We serve really satisfying food, and do whatever it takes to make it. That's what we draw upon. A satifying environment, and satisfying interpersonal relationships with our staff.

Care

I like to think that I have a real sensitivity to the way I think people want their food, and want their restaurant to be—even if *they've* never thought about it themselves. This is especially true in the way food is prepared. Cooking eggs gently instead of just murdering them on the grill. That's how I insist we do it, and so that's how we do it.

Restaurant food tends to be churned out these days, and in the process it is massacred. Eggs are rubbery. Bread things are overcooked, or made from a mix in which you can actually taste the chemicals. Somehow just the fact that a locally made muffin is on the table is supposed to merit a round of applause.

But it shouldn't. We've got all these shlocky food manufacturers out there, who turn out tremendous quantities of complete garbage. Mass production has its advantages, sure, but that doesn't mean Twinkies for the World is good. The homecooked approach, whether done in a home or in a small restaurant, is the worthy one.

We've been discovering over the past ten or fifteen years that it is the company or restaurant that turns out perfectly made items that really has a handle on what it's all about. Generally, the quantities are small. We have only thirty-eight seats, and I'm quite certain that we could never do as good a job if we were much larger. Many of our suppliers are small, too. I can't imagine what our maple syrup supplier would do if we asked for 500 gallons instead of the 5 we buy each week.

So if the product tastes good, and *is* good (the two are not always synonymous, thanks to the wonders of modern food chemistry), and is made by people who care about it, then there will be clients who care about it, too.

Breakfast

We are, basically, a breakfast restaurant that also does lunches and, for part of the year, dinners. Breakfast is a significant meal in a number of respects. For one thing, people rarely eat good well-prepared breakfasts, whether in restaurants, or in their own homes. Yet when people reminisce about happy times in their lives, they associate breakfast with Mom and the comforts of home and fresh orange juice and great coffee and warmth and friendly people and all that. But how often does this happen any more?

I think many people are cranky at breakfast time because they've just gotten up, and there is no one to squeeze the oranges and make them perfect pancakes and warm the syrup and cook the eggs exactly the way they like them. When they discover that this is exactly what we do, they tend to grow extremely content, even before the salmon omelette (page 182) appears before them.

Toute notre Pâtisserie est Garantie au Beurre

Choices

Aside from choosing your steak rare, medium or well done, there are very few times in a restaurant when you get to specify exactly how you want your food prepared—especially with any expectation of getting it that way.

At Cafe Beaujolais, we don't put up signs saying, "Tell us exactly how to cook your meal." Most of the time, what seems right to me also seems right to the customers. But whenever people ask for a two-egg omelette (or in the case of one regular, a 1½-egg omelette) or for their scrambled eggs to be cooked just so, for more or fewer sausages or whatever it may be, within reason (or not too far outside reason), if we can, we'll oblige.

One reason we can do this, of course, is our size. I like the idea and the feeling of a small dining room, and the level of quality and flexibility I can maintain. Even though I would prefer the money I could make with a larger room, it would be a different kind of restaurant, and one I would not be nearly as happy running. (Besides, I keep reminding myself on those winter Wednesdays when there are three people in the dining room at 10 a.m., if I had more than thirty-eight seats, I'd simply have more empty ones.)

Magic

Well maybe *not* magic. But there's *some*thing going on that's hard to explain—and we primitive rustics traditionally apply the word "magic" to things we don't readily understand.

My first job in Mendocino was baking bread at the Mendocino Hotel. I turned out hundreds of loaves a week. What struck me so was people's appreciation of that product. It wasn't the bread itself, as much as the way they seemed to enjoy eating it. It was as if it had to do with the collective unconscious memory of food production and home and family and all kinds of positive images.

People responded to the bread—as they do to the breakfasts at the restaurant—with such heartfelt feelings, their experience went way beyond whatever they were eating at that moment.

And that's one of the psychologically satisfying aspects of what I'm doing. Even if people don't stop to think about what they're liking—even when they can't identify what exactly is so pleasant about the experience, they know it is good, and that makes me feel good.

When customers and reviewers use the term "home cooking," to me that doesn't just stand for steak and a baked potato and Mom's apple pie. "Home" is a way of life, something satisfying that you feel comfortable with. That's one reason it's really important to me to keep the restaurant small and accessible. We're not big and flashy and we never will be. I want us always to be able to respond to people on a one-to-one basis, whether they're in the dining room, or writing a letter of praise or inquiry or even a complaint.

This role doesn't come easily. We have to work at it all the time. I've never met anyone fussier than I am. This is *not* an easy place to work, in that both the standards and the expectations are high. It's the only way I know how to do things. I am regularly surprised by the amount of mediocrity in the world.

When regular customers or staff have been away for a while, and then they return, they invariably say, "You know, the food is *awful* out there. I had no idea it was going to be like that."

That makes me feel good. It means that they appreciate Cafe Beaujolais in a way they didn't before. And it means they have accepted and integrated these high standards into their ordinary way of life. They have come to expect that level of performance. People *should* have high expectations; otherwise they're doomed to wallow in the mediocrity that is so rampant these days—a sort of plodding, bland acceptance of what goes on, maybe with some whining in the back.

But that isn't how things get great. I think there is a close parallel here with those parents who learn that children really *do* want some order and discipline and structure in their lives—even if they *say* they don't.

Last year, one of our regular customers brought his mother here for her eightieth birthday. They were seated

"I've worked here on and off for three or four years. As a janitor, I've learned that this is a very nice place at night when no one's here and it's dark. It's very beautiful with the light coming through the windows and no one here but the cat. During the day, the people seem very happy—both the staff and the customers. It's a nice place for me to come into. It's something I look forward to, and one doesn't always look forward to one's work."
—Cafe Beaujolais Janitor

These premises are protected by a

watch cat

on the deck, and he told his waiter why he was ordering wine (locals don't order wine very much). When the waiter brought the wine, he set it down, and proceeded to sing, "If I Were a Rich Man" to her. Here was this man, this loving face with big happy eyes, singing his heart out for an elderly lady, and all the customers just sat there waiting for their breakfasts and thinking how wonderful it was. Can you imagine if this happened in the city? I envision irritated customers thinking, "What kind of weirdo is doing this? And why isn't he bringing me my omelette?"

Now things like this are charming in their way, but the important thing is that they are logical pieces of a much larger whole. When you have a certain kind of place—a certain style—then all these nice things happen that seem ordinary, or at least unexceptional to me, but really impress others.

Especially for out-of-towners, there's that element of surprise, that feeling of serendipity. Here they are, three hours from the real world, and they stumble into this old yellow house. It's pleasantly decorated, but it won't ever win any awards. We've got a bumpy floor that always seems to need a new wax job. But they discover a rather large menu, and there's real maple syrup and pure unsalted butter, and the muffins are made from scratch, and they just happened to fall into a nice experience—even if we don't always have arias on the deck.

Style

That's one of those things that you know when you see, but it's hard to write about. Essentially I think of it as everything being of a piece. The food. The wallpaper. The attitudes of the staff. The absence of microwave ovens and fluorescent lights. The fact that letters get personal answers. Lucy, the cat, who gets steamed half and half every morning, and shrimp or paté many afternoons.

It is crucially important for me that I do something that I can really feel good about. It is much more important to live every single day feeling complete and congruent about what you're doing, instead of being a schlub most of your

life and then hoping that when you retire, you can make it all worthwhile.

It's like never taking a real vacation, and saving it all up for a big trip when you're sixty-two. What about maintaining a quality of life for the first sixty-one years, whatever form it may have taken.

So that's why I've done things which may have seemed foolish from a business standpoint. But for my own personal standards, I've known they were right. For instance, I spent money on graphics and design when there wasn't money to spend. Bought exactly the right wallpaper (which wasn't cheap) when there may have been more pressing bills to pay.

But then people say, "I love your stationery," or they like the way you did this or that, and I know that in the long run, what I did was good for business as well as for my soul. I live my life as I go along. I don't save it all up for some uncertain future time.

I remember reading that when Xerox Corporation donated millions of dollars to the United Nations, they got a lot of flak from some stockholders. "What are you doing to our profits," they clamored. Xerox replied that their U.N. support was not only good for humanity, but in the long run was going to be good for business. Sure enough, years later their sales in Third World countries are booming, in large measure because of their political stance in the '60s.

And so, as I explain to my accountant (who worries about such things), it may not be cost effective to use pure maple syrup. So our profit per waffle (PPW, we say in the trade) may not be up to industry-wide standards, but our repeat business, and our word-of-mouth business, and our reputation will keep on growing as a result of this, and a hundred other things like it—and in the long run, I know that's good for business.

THE FOOD

Why There Are No Menus in This Book

Yes, I know that some very successful and popular recent cookbooks have been based on menus. But there aren't menus in here because I don't think I'd want to follow anybody else's menu.

I am a firm believer in putting together whatever in the world you want. Why do you need someone else, whatever their credentials, to tell you that this entrée only goes with tomatoes and that one only with green beans? I believe there is magic in the perfect blend of flavors and intensities, but I would never presuppose to tell anyone else what *their* magic must be.

There are places in this book where I do say, for instance, that White Bean Goop (see page 164) goes especially well with lamb. But for goodness' sakes, if you wanted to serve it with sausages or roast beef or "tuna surprise", please feel free.

We all have our own feelings about what seems right. For me, if I had a cream soup and then a steak prepared with *foie gras* sauce, potatoes and a rich salad, I'd never serve a chocolate dessert. That would be overkill. Yet I see people eating exactly like that at the restaurant, and loving it all the way. Just because *I* wouldn't want to eat like that, there's no reason why you shouldn't.

Perhaps some readers want that kind of regimentation. They want the Experts On High to tell them just what to eat with what else, and what things don't go with what other things. Sorry, you don't get that from me. All you get is the encouragement that it's all right to experiment. Break your chains. Mix ingredients and dishes as you wish. Experiment by varying recipes, ingredients, techniques. I give you *carte blanche* to try whatever you want. Just don't blame me if everything goes wrong.

Making Mistakes

Many people tell me that they could never run a restaurant. They are even reluctant to have an elegant dinner party at home, for fear of making mistakes. It is as if they had to turn out perfect meals (whatever *that* may mean) every time, and the fear of failure paralyzes them into inactivity.

You've got to be willing to try. If the bread doesn't come out, that isn't the end of the world. We've had breads that just didn't rise. We've worked long and hard and ended up with a dreadful veal dish. Nobody cooks 100% perfectly all the time. And even if *you* think something is 100% perfect, the next guy who comes along doesn't like his crust like that, or thinks it's too salty, or not salty enough. You can never please everybody.

The first important thing is to go out and learn by experimentation. The second important thing is to start with good ingredients, and have the guts to keep on trying things until *you're* happy. That's my advice to everybody.

When I was seventeen and eighteen, I taught bread-baking classes at the Unitarian Church in Kensington. I remember so vividly that people would tentatively poke at this lump of dough that really wanted to be thrashed about wildly. I said, "Come on, touch it, beat it—that's what makes the dough become what you want." They said, "Oh, I don't want to hurt it."

I tried to convince them that they were hurting it more by not touching it than they ever would by smacking it around. It was wonderful to see them finally picking it up and throwing it down on the counter. They finally came to realize that you can knead bread dough into oblivion and it will only keep getting better.

Being Creative

Psychologists have been arguing for decades over whether creativity can be taught, much less measured. Happily, in the home kitchen, it hardly matters. Some people are content to follow recipes exactly, work crossword puzzles, and take guided tours. Others experiment with food combinations, write short stories, and hitchhike across the Outback. It's absurd to say one is better than the other; just different.

I find that there are at least three kinds of approaches I take to waxing creative in the kitchen, in the sense of creating new (or at least new-to-me) dishes: blank canvases, simple substitutions, and building on an ingredient.

1. The "Blank Canvas" approach: Certain dishes are so simple, so uncluttered, that they just sit there begging for creative addenda. Three excellent examples are crêpes, pasta, and omelettes. There is no end to the fillings and sauces with which you can paint these canvases. Hot or cold. Spicy or mild. Sweet or sour. Chunky or smooth. On and on. Some examples are given in these pages (182, 188, 202 for instance), and they are quite interchangeable. It is hard to imagine something that could successfully fill an omelette that wouldn't also work well in a crêpe or as the basis for a pasta sauce.

2. Simple substitutions: If you have a successful recipe, the odds are high that if you replace one or two ingredients with others that are somewhat similar, you will have another successful recipe. The substitutions can be simple and logical (walnuts for cashews); simple and illogical (candied cherries for chocolate chips); or as complex as you wish. There are probably no two foods that explode when mixed together, so the worst that can happen is a culinary disaster, and not a destroyed kitchen.

I'm always willing to try changing things. I'm not the sort of person who says, "For the past 400 years, this has been made with strawberries, therefore I can never use raspberries." If it tastes good, then it's valid. Completely valid. A recipe doesn't have to win points on the Escoffier Scale in order to be acceptable.

3. Building on an ingredient: This is where many of my recipes come from. I start with some element of a dish that appeals to me. For example, I might begin by thinking how the flakiness of a pie crust or tart dough is particularly excellent, and wouldn't that be good with . . . something. So I start making associations. I'm a member of the less-sugar-is-better crowd, so my desserts tend to be less sweet than many. (I think a lot of people would be completely content sucking on a sugar cube for dessert.)

I have a strong curiosity about the way some food items seem to complement others. That dough with a fruit. Two fruits. A vegetable? The line between categories is often faint. Yams as a dessert; pineapple with an entrée. That sort of thing. Sometimes I'll go through this process only in my head, or on paper. Other times, I'll go into the laboratory, as it were. What *would* an unsweetened tart crust taste like filled with sun-dried tomatoes? And so on.

Admittedly, it is much easier to do this kind of thing when you own a restaurant. There are so many foodstuffs to play around with. It's not as if you're home and if you want to try something with walnuts, you've got to go out and spend money. I've always got all the nuts and chocolates and other goods I want, so it is very conducive to being adventuresome. But anyone can be creative with excess foods and leftovers.

Regarding Leftovers

There are restaurant management textbooks that say the difference between a profitable and an unprofitable operation often lies in the area of leftover management. The same can probably be said for the home kitchen as well.

We've never been faced with monumental recycling problems at the restaurant, which is a testament to the fact that we plan things pretty darn carefully. You might say that the best way to deal with leftovers is to figure out how not to have any.

Restaurant leftovers are almost always recyclable in a legal and satisfactory fashion. Of course we don't re-use food from people's plates (except to feed the cat).

When we have surplus vegetables, I like cooking them very plainly, or blanching them, currying them, and using them in an omelette. Curry is a nice way to turn all kinds of leftovers into something different from whatever the original may have been.

For example, we might add curry to a cream of chicken soup and serve it the next day as curried cream of chicken soup. (Be sure to remove the raw taste of curry by cooking it over medium heat for two or three minutes with an equal amount of butter, then stirring it into the soup.)

Leftovers provide a great opportunity to make a spontaneous soup of any type. I'm told that some kitchens actually have leftover tomatoes (I generally finish them off myself). I'd purée them, strain them, add some cream, and make a tomato soup. Or perhaps cut them up fine and combine them with other vegetables for an omelette or crêpe filling.

As previously indicated, omelette and crêpe fillings offer ample opportunities for creative leftover management. One Sunday morning, I had a ton of vegetables on hand. Zucchini, tomatoes, green beans. I blanched them, sautéed them with a lot of herbs and garlic. I threw in a tub of Herbed Cream Cheese (see page 189), and some cooked bacon. It all melted into a sauce that was so delicious in the omelette—much more than the sum of the parts.

Finally, another advantage to having a restaurant is using leftovers for the staff meals. If we only have a few portions of salmon left, we wouldn't put it on the menu, but it makes great staff meals.

Regarding Cookbooks

I read them constantly for pleasure. I enjoy getting a new one and just sitting down and reading it all the way through. My mother has a gigantic collection—more than 2,000, I think, not including the bags of recipes in the closet, and her complete collection of *Sunset* magazines back to the year one. I vowed that I would never engage in that sort of behavior. Who wants to be a second legend in the same family? But now there are times when I see the restaurant as being nothing more than a legitimate reason for engaging in *exactly* that sort of behavior.

What does my mother do with 2,000 cookbooks, I hear you wondering. She spends a lot of time comparing. If I mention to her that I'd like to make an apple pie, she will get out fifteen or twenty recipes, and compare and contrast them—this crust versus that crust, and with brown sugar or white sugar or honey or Ritz crackers, and don't I remember the pie she made when I was four in Los Angeles because I said I really liked it then.

My mom often has so many comparisons going that she doesn't end up making very many things. Even when she does—this is a behavior I found hard to understand, but a lot of people seem to engage in it—she seems content to make something once, no matter how wonderfully it turns out. She made a spectacular Dobosh Torte for my first birthday (there is photographic evidence), but never another. She loves the intellectual challenge, and once it is done, she's completed her task and doesn't have to do it again.

I will follow a recipe religiously the first time through—well, maybe a few minor substitutions here and there—but after that, it's improvisation city.

When interviewers ask me, as is their wont, which are my favorite cookbooks (or, more dramatically, which ones

I would save if my house were burning down and I could only rescue a few), my honest answer is that I don't think I'd really care. I'd leave them all behind. There is no one book that is so important to me, I couldn't get through tomorrow without it.

I do like Julia Child's cookbooks. I'm always intrigued by Maida Heatter's books, especially her *Great Desserts*. I love Barbara Tropp's *Modern Art of Chinese Cooking* because it makes this exotic cuisine so accessible to me. I also like Richard Sax's *Cooking Great Meals Every Day*.

The old *Time-Life* cookbooks from the '60s are wonderful. Great photographs on classical French cooking. As for people writing about food, there is no one better than M.F.K. Fisher and Calvin Trillin.

STARTING A
RESTAURANT

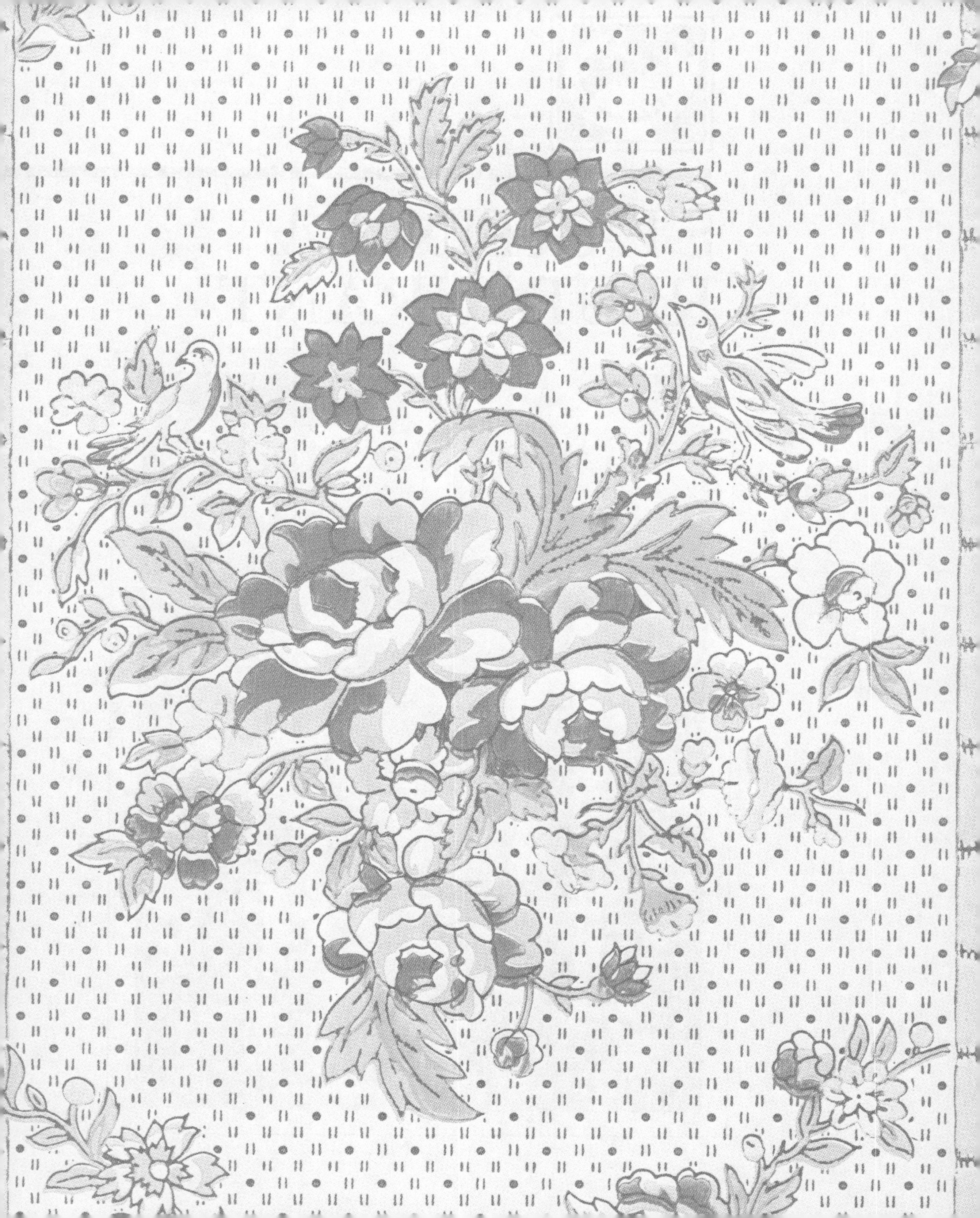

I can't imagine why anyone would want to. It made perfectly good sense to me at the time, but my reasons were so personal, it's hard to see how they could have relevance for others. The amount of work involved is huge. And the financial rewards (if any),as I shall discuss later, are rarely substantial.

But if the idea won't go away, then the important questions to ask, probably in this order, are these:

1. Do I want to (and can I) run a business of *any* kind?
2. If so, should that business be a restaurant?
3. If so, should it be a country restaurant?

Needless to say, that's not the way most people do it, and it's certainly not the way I did it long ago in 1976.

Actually, my parents and sister remember that restaurants were on my mind even when I was fourteen. My sister Emily and I used to sit around talking about how someday we would open a restaurant, and because I love the early morning and breakfast, it would be primarily a breakfast restaurant. I loved that idea when I was fourteen, and I love it now. Like so many things at Cafe Beaujolais, what happened came about simply because I like it that way, and that's all there is to it.

Besides the teenage restaurant fantasy, I always had a very powerful feeling that I would accomplish something that meant a lot to me before I was twenty-five.

So there I was in Mendocino, where I'd gone for an allegedly short stay after college, baking bread at the Hotel, making food at The Cheese Shop, and doing some baking for this little restaurant owned by Ellen and Gerald Pitsenbarger. They founded it, and had been running it for eight or nine years, and then, just about the time I was thinking about what to do next, they put it up for sale.

I knew very little about running any kind of a business, much less a restaurant, but somehow it seemed the right thing to do. The Pitsenbargers closed on New Year's Eve 1976. With two partners, I opened for business four months later, on April 28, 1977. I was twenty-four.

I was also alarmingly undercapitalized, woefully naive, highly competitive, and almost terminally stubborn. The first two nearly did me in. The last two kept (and keep) me going.

According to some how-to-run-a-business books I've glanced at, undercapitalization is one of the three main reasons new businesses fail. Poor record-keeping is another. Personnel problems is a third. In the early days, weeks, years, I had some of each. Indeed, for many good reasons, the restaurant should never have succeeded.

Loans from my family, close friends, and the bank helped us through the early money problems. I soon became convinced that I was the only partner who clearly saw what the responsibilities and demands of being in this business were—and was willing to meet them. By the end of the second year, I had bought out my partners.

In retrospect, the crucial factor in the very difficult early years was the fact that I owned the real estate as well as the business. It had so much more meaning for me, psychologically and emotionally. If I hadn't owned it, and could have just closed up the doors and walked away, I would have been more likely to abandon ship. There were probably a fair number of times when I would have done just that. But I had obligations. Mortgage payments. A huge investment of time and energy.

Even so, each year when I did my taxes, I thought seriously about selling out. For years, I simply did not make any money. In the first four years, I probably averaged about $250 a month, or less than a dollar an hour for the time I spent. That's hardly something to aim for as a goal, as my parents often reminded me, with variations of the "For this we put you through college?" speech.

This is where my stubborn streak saved the day. The idea of selling just overwhelmed me. It was inconceivable that something into which I'd put so much of myself wasn't going to make it. I knew that I could not continue to live in Mendocino if anybody else owned that restaurant. I had (and have) such a strong idea of what I wanted the restaurant to be; what its potential was. The incentive to work even harder, to learn even more, was so strong.

In starting a restaurant, it is essential to understand and deal with three things: money, people, and psychology. A few words on each.

Money: This is so simple to say, and it is so easy to ignore. If I were starting a restaurant today, I would delve deeply and *realistically* into the costs. What will it *really* take to run the enterprise? And I don't mean, oh yeah, if everything's on our side, and the economy doesn't decline and our seats are 90% occupied all year and no staff members ever leave.

Fairy tale economics doesn't work. Figure the worst of everything, and if you have half a chance of struggling through with enough money to provide operating capital and a cushion, then you may have a chance. It's not fun to work for years for a dollar an hour.

People: Running a restaurant is an extremely labor intensive business. It takes a lot of people to make things work, and there is typically a very high turnover (a problem we thankfully don't have). There is a strong temptation to say things like, "Well I can't really afford an extra waiter just now; the ones I have can work a little harder." Often this is a big mistake; you just can't neglect service.

And there are all those delightful aspects of dealing with the public. Being there and relatively cheerful every single day, no matter how you feel. Coping with complaints and cancellations and late deliveries and on and on. In the course of one summer month, I'll have seven or eight thousand customers—and end up with the same revenues that a car dealer would get in dealing with less than a dozen customers. It's a very different way of life, of earning a living, and you've got to be ready for it.

Psychology: It's a high pressure business. Many people think of restaurant as theater. We've got to be there and be absolutely ready every day at 8:00 in the morning when the curtain goes up. The group that has driven sixty miles for breakfast doesn't find it charming that the power is out so they can't have waffles. They want, and have a right to, the performance.

There is small-scale pressure all day long. Each of 200 to 300 meals has to be right. When I put an omelette up on the bridge and ring my little bell and it isn't picked up in a few seconds, I begin to grow testy. I want every part of this day's performance to be perfect, which means no plates cooling off, ever.

The positive side of restaurant-as-theater is the pleasure we give people. We're constantly putting on a show—the ambience, the flowers, the amiability, and of course the food. When the customers are happy (which is, for us, a lot of the time), then I am happy.

I don't expect to have ulcers by the time I'm forty, but I read that all too many restaurant owners and managers do.

Where Are You Going to Do It?

It is, I think, widely believed that about 73% of the families who live in or near big cities harbor the fantasy that one day they will escape to the country and open up a little restaurant. With Mom's famous recipes and Pop's business skills (or vice versa, as the case may be), it's a natural.

Well, maybe. It depends so much on your goals, one of which must not be making a fortune. Just because you can cook and add doesn't mean you can run a business.

People come to Mendocino (and other tourist areas) during the summer, observe the village full of people, lines waiting to get into restaurants, crowded sidewalks, bulging boutiques, and the like. Visions of dollar signs begin to dance in their heads. There should be a law requiring these people to return for a series of cold and rainy Tuesdays in January when the number of tourists can sometimes be counted on the fingers of one finger and many small businesspeople are studying their bankbooks and counting the days until Easter weekend.

Our tourist association issues a little town map each spring, showing the locations of all businesses. I indulged in the exercise of comparing this year's map with the one from five years ago. I discovered the depressing statistic that more than 70% of the businesses—restaurants, galleries, boutiques, ice cream parlors, shoe stores, pizza parlors, computer stores, and so forth—had not survived five years. One major reason in almost all cases, I'd venture, was simply lack of clientele.

For me, though, the tradeoff is worth it. I'll never have a huge and immensely profitable restaurant, but I get to live in a beautiful place, with no smog, no traffic, and none of that intense level of competition that I would have if I were one of 4,000 restaurants in San Francisco instead of one of five or six in Mendocino.

I can summarize all that I wish I had known in eight words: study hard, don't undercapitalize, and hire good people. Those last three words refer as much to advisors as to kitchen staff. We have learned the importance of dealing with the best lawyers and accountants we can find. Ours happen to be in far-off San Francisco. We pay a pretty penny, but we have terrific systems and, I remain convinced, good advice. It's one thing to be a little rustic rural villagey restaurant, but you don't necessarily want rustic rural villagey financial or business advisors.

The quality of my life certainly took a turn for the better when I hired a full-time manager, Patricia Priano, a couple of years ago. It was one of those situations where the economics said I couldn't afford to, but common sense said I couldn't afford *not* to, and it was a great decision.

Finally, reflect deeply and long on whether you would rather live in the city, breathe smog, triple lock your door every night, and make X dollars; or live in the country, breathe air, rarely lock anything, and make Y dollars, where Y is a good deal less than X. There are no simple answers, and the only foolish answers are those that are made in haste without considering all the ramifications.

RUNNING A
RESTAURANT

This is not a text on starting and running a restaurant. There are, of course, books available on the subject, but none of them is the definitive "Bible" of restaurant running, where you can turn to page 843 and get the precise answer you need to this morning's problem. Also, and significantly, they all seem to start with "How to . . . " rather than addressing the essential question of "Should you?"

People find it very hard to accept or understand how much trial and error, not to mention blood, sweat and tears, went into creating this package called Cafe Beaujolais that, after seven years, is running relatively smoothly. And even "running smoothly" doesn't mean we don't still have plenty of problems. But we've learned how to think on our feet and deal with the problems as they occur.

People are baffled by the realization, or perhaps the revelation that there is no one perfect way to start and run a restaurant; that things do get put together rather haphazardly; and that things that work in one place won't necessarily work elsewhere.

It's a constant pattern of evolving or inventing new parts to replace old parts when they don't fit in, or break down, or don't seem right any more. There is no straight path to follow. You don't hire the musicians, put them together, and expect the orchestra to play right the first time.

In this section, I'm going to discuss many of the relevant issues and meta-issues related to starting and running a restaurant. By "issue," I mean the nitty-gritty specifics, ranging from choosing menu items to cleaning bathrooms, dealing with bad checks, and to handling unruly customers. By "meta-issue," I mean matters dealing with personality and psychology and life in general: anxiety, flexibility, personal satisfaction and so forth.

But to begin with, permit me to describe just what I actually do on a typical day. I've spoken to people who have the romantic idea that a restaurant ownership consists of dropping by in the afternoon, sipping an aperitif, cheering the staff on, counting the receipts, and heading home. There may be owners like that out there somewhere. I've never met one—but then I'm usually back in the kitchen working like the dickens.

"A friend of mine was in Mendocino last week, and was so impressed by the smooth efficiency of the restaurant. It was in the morning, and the place was crowded. Then she walked around the outside and looked in the door, and there was Margaret at the stove, dancing to that crazy music they sometimes play in the back, while she was doing whatever she was doing at the stove. My friend thought that was great, that this could be happening under duress. You know, the kitchen is really a very stressful place. But I thought it was all quite nice."

—Anne Fox

A Typical Day at Cafe Beaujolais

I get up at about 5:45 a.m. in order to be at the restaurant by 6:30 at the latest. I'm usually the first one there, and I like it that way. Somehow everything seems as if it's slipping out of my control, my clutches, if I'm not there first to survey the territory. I'll start by turning on all the lights, of course, and plugging in the espresso machine.

Then I start to figure out what specials I'm going to offer that day: the special omelette, and the special breakfast. Usually that's a fairly spontaneous decision. It's not anything I've belabored over the past three weeks, wondering and planning what to serve on that particular Wednesday morning.

I start the process leading to my decisions by looking in the walk-in refrigerator and seeing what I've got. I start by pulling out the regular items, the things that are always on the menu. Then there are always some little extras. There might be some leftover salmon from a previous special, or extra vegetables that I could curry and combine to make an omelette. There might be a large number of stale baguettes so I could feature French toast. With a huge quantity of overly ripe bananas, I would conclude that we have to make banana muffins or perhaps Mom's Banana Cake (see page 213). Something along that line.

While I'm pondering and planning, other people begin arriving. We have groggy greetings (it's still only about 7:00, after all), and I'll discuss my thoughts and plans with the others—especially the prep cook.

The prep cook is responsible, among other things, for the baking, salad preparation, sandwiches, and the "set-ups" for the things that I do. For example, when a hamburger order comes in, I call for a hamburger set-up. The prep arranges the plate with the lettuce, tomatoes and bun. I cook the meat and put it on the (usually) waiting set-up.

The prep cook will tell me what it is that he or she would like to "get rid of" today. There may be left over cooked salmon that can go into a luncheon salad. There

may be a surplus of Herbed Cream Cheese, which we can use up in an omelette (see page 189).

So, for about ten or fifteen minutes, there's a great deal of communication and planning going on. By 7:15, the waiting staff has arrived, and I'm in conference with them about any of the out-of-the-ordinary jobs to be done.

By 7:45, potatoes are cooking, the grill is turned on, and all the electrical appliances are being readied for their use when the doors open in fifteen minutes. The waiting staff is always babying us a little around this time—offering to make us espresso drinks—and we love it.

So there are two or three of us in the kitchen. We are always playing music by this time. What kind of music? Well, it depends who gets to the tape machine first. Frequently it is loud and raucous; something with a beat, to drum activity into our blood. If it's too genteel and charming, I'll raise a hue and cry lest I start to fall asleep. Sometimes one simply *needs* an injection of Stevie Wonder.

Now that I know what the specials are going to be, I write them on the blackboards, and review them with the staff, so everyone will be able to talk about them intelligently to the public. When I'm done, the prep cook pretty much repeats my performance, but he or she will mention anything we especially want to "push" because we've got a lot of it on hand.

This is the time when good communication is essential. Sometimes we have dishes that might not sound as wonderful as they really are, and the waiting staff needs to know, either by tasting or by getting a pep talk, just how good they are. Fried mush is a splendid example of this (page 196).

We go over portion size—how large a piece or how many pieces of something represent a serving. We review the specials one more time, and by now it's 7:55 and time to put on music more appropriate to the dining room: either classical or jazz.

The prep cook and I have our final consultation to be sure we're both ready (we always say we are). If the espresso machine is also ready (it always is), then, with little fanfare, we open the doors.

If it's a Sunday, a crowd of people will be huddling outside, and we can expect to be nearly full and very busy from the opening gun. But most weekdays, things begin calmly and quietly. In fact, it's usually not until 9:00 that we start getting busy. Oh, to be sure, there are miscellaneous orders coming in for the first hour, but people don't tend to eat a lot of food at that early hour. They don't have three-egg omelettes with fried potatoes and a side of toast. Orders are easy to handle, and the cooking fits in nicely with the prep work being done at the same time.

Prep work includes anything from breaking eggs to grating cheese to making the lunch soup to organizing the lunch special. Many functions occur on an overlapping basis. I always get in some housekeeping—walking into the walk-in to see what needs to be disposed of, replaced, or used.

The dishwasher arrives around 8:30 as the first dirty

dishes are accumulating. My manager arrives around 9:00, and by then we have a good idea of how busy a day it is going to be. If necessary, we can call for more staff to come in and help out: a busser, a third waitress if we decide to open the deck, etc. On a busy morning, we may have eight or nine people at work, which is quite a few for a thirty-eight-seat restaurant.

By 9:00 a.m., I like to know that lunch is under control. It's asking for trouble if you think, "Oh, I've got plenty of time; I'll start thinking about lunch when the breakfast crowd thins out." Inevitably, that will be the day that seventy-four people decide to have a late breakfast, and if it gets close to 11:00 and you're not all ready for lunch, you're going to be in a lot of trouble.

Lunch starts at 11:30, and all hell breaks loose if you don't have enough time to get it all together in a well-planned fashion. Also, if you are frantically trying to get lunch together in a big rush, it interjects a level of anxiety into the process that hurts everyone and everything. It's frantic enough without this.

One of the complicating things about our schedule is that breakfast continues all day, with lunch overlapping it, starting at 11:30. It would be much less complicated if we ended breakfast and began lunch, because the rhythms of those two meals are very different. Also, there are processes that are not very compatible. For instance, in the past, when we got a French toast order (see page 191) and a hamburger order at the same time, we had to be especially careful not to produce hamburger-grease-flavored French toast on our one and only grill. We finally solved that problem by taking French toast off the menu at 11:30.

As the morning progresses, then, the lunch soup is made, heated, and put out in the front station for the waitresses. We go through the same discussions about the lunch specials, reviewing them for the waiting staff. This time, however, the work has to be done in and among their activities of serving their customers.

It is rare for lunch orders to start immediately at 11:30, but by 12:00 or 12:15 we're totally into lunch, while con-

"The reason the Cafe Beaujolais is the best place in the state to start the day is because its owner, Margaret Fox, is one of the few people around who know how to cook eggs."
—Ruth Reichl, Restaurant Critic *California Magazine*

tinuing with breakfast. We've got our momentum up by then, and we play out the orders for the rest of the shift, until we close the doors at 2:30 p.m.

But the business end goes on. Deliveries normally begin at 1:00 typically with, say, seventy-five pounds of cheese plonked down right in front of the refrigerator door. We have a small kitchen. Things have to be moved around, and we have to move ourselves around things. It seems there is much less freedom than there was five or six hours earlier.

Finally, just when we think it's never going to end, it ends. The staff puts in their own food orders around 2:15 or 2:30. We cook their meals, and then we start cleaning up and putting everything away. Magically, the kitchen goes back to looking as it did when we first walked in—a feat which always seems impossible at the height of the earlier chaos.

And so we start planning for the next day. You always have to think ahead. You should always prep as if you knew you were going to be sick and not come in and some-one else is going to be called in to do the job. You want to leave everything at the end of the day so that anyone who is reasonably well-qualified can come in the next day and do the job, if necessary. Afternoon prepping includes crack-ing eggs, grating cheese, washing and cutting vegetables, and possibly starting tomorrow's soup.

The last customers are gone by 3:30. The staff has fin-ished eating by then, too. We all clean our respective places, the staff goes home, and I start the other part of my day's work.

People ask me, "But what do you actually *do* then?" The simplest answer is paperwork. Immense amounts of pa-perwork. There are letters to be answered; somebody wants a recipe (which we usually provide—although now we can just tell them to buy this book!); there is advertis-ing to place. Do I want to make an appearance, do a public demonstration or take part in a wine-tasting event. Public relations is so important, and all these matters must be handled with care and politeness.

I used to do it all. Cooking every day, and paperwork until 7:00 or 8:00 in the evening. Finally, after about four years of being constantly behind and constantly worn out, I came to accept the impossibility of ever getting it all done. So at the present time, I'm only cooking two or three days a week, and my manager deals with a lot of the paperwork and staff issues.

And I've sort of made a promise to myself that I'll leave by 4:30 or 5:00. I really want to leave while it's still light. I hate to arrive in the dark and leave in the dark. That's one of the reasons I've been closing for a couple of months in mid-winter. It's tremendously depressing never to see the sunlight.

So now it's a mere ten to eleven-hour workday—seven days a week. But I'm not complaining. What keeps it from being a grind is that the job is made up of so many different facets. It's not as if I'm standing on an assembly line sticking something into something else a thousand times an hour. I'm dealing with people (who can be both interesting and irritating at the same time), and I'm dealing with food, and I'm dealing with business. There is always a certain level of excitement and energy which really appeals to me.

Sometimes I'm embarrassed when I admit to these seventy- to eighty-hour weeks. I know you're supposed to delegate work, and find more time for yourself. But whenever I try to do this—and I have very competent people to delegate work to—I don't quite know what to do with my free time. I only seem to relax when I'm actually physically away from Mendocino where I cannot be involved.

I *love* this restaurant. I *love* to be here seven days a week. I just like being around this place.

So on many days I'll have an early dinner and go home. When we're serving dinners at the restaurant during the summer, I may hang around and do the drinks, or work the espresso machine, or be the cashier. I like it. But I start fading dramatically around 8:00 in the evening. I force myself to go home, I may read a little, write some letters, and then I'll get to sleep early, having set my alarm for 5:45 the next morning.

On Anxiety

This is an anxiety-ridden business. Even if you enjoy it, as I do, there is a very fine line between anxiety and exhilaration. The way I think of it is that I have this building, these four walls. Everything is going to happen within this space. I've got to figure out how things will work best in this given space. It's like a huge three-dimensional puzzle, with frequently changing and ever shifting pieces.

If you like that, then it *is* exhilarating with only a tinge of anxiety. If you don't, the emotions are reversed and you'll be eaten alive.

Sometimes I have to remind myself that I'm in this because I like it. I cannot afford, emotionally, psychically, functionally or any other way, to get angry or upset every time something doesn't work. I must accept the fact that the dishwashing apparatus is going to break down, and try not to say, "Oh, damn it," and go flying off the handle at whoever happens to be walking by at that moment.

Everything has to flow. There's this huge and complex machine, and it simply *has* to flow. I can't think of any other field, except perhaps show business, that combines as much pressure and tension with as much excitement and pizzazz. And it tastes good, too.

People who hang around for a while often say, "Oh, how do you ever stand all that pandemonium? It must be so confusing, and so this and so that." On the contrary, that's what people who are involved in the restaurant business do like. They like the fact that it's show time every morning at 8:00 when the doors open.

There's always an interesting blend of camaraderie and tension. An outside observer seeing the intensity with which I pound on my little bell, or demand a set-up plate, may think that I am genuinely distressed or tyrannical or both. Maybe for those few seconds I am—but the staff knows that we all go through a very large range of feelings and emotions during the day. That's OK as long as we keep a basic equilibrium. But if we constantly have to be what we're not, that's when things start shredding.

Quite simply, the tension, and the high level of anxiety, never go away. Unless you can stand it, and go on from there, you're in the wrong business.

On Flexibility

We maintain an almost alarming level of flexibility. But when we bend, it is invariably in the direction of doing even more for our customers.

For instance, people are just not used to the notion of finding a restaurant that is willing to make things that aren't on the menu, or to modify those things that are. I know that some people don't come here because they find our regular portions too large. It never occurs to them that they can order a two-egg or even, I suppose, a one-egg ome-lette, or a half order of almost anything. We are almost always willing to accommodate people's wishes.

Same thing with our hours. For much of the year, we're open from 8:00 to 2:30, but once a couple called and said they were on their way from some distant point and would be late, we just stayed open for them. Of course if we had known that they would get bogged down in highway construction, be 2½ hours late, and have only soup and salad once they arrived, we might possibly have responded differently.

The one thing we cannot do, and maintain a professional stance, is to be flexible in ways that suit our needs, but disregard our customers'. For example, when things are so slow by 1:00 p.m., there's an almost overwhelming temptation to close early. There are dark and stormy winter mornings when, if we opened half an hour later, the earth would not shift in its orbit. But we simply would never do those things. We open and close at the proper times no matter what.

It's the same with cooking. If something is printed on the menu, we'll do everything in our power to have it there and ready, in spite of late deliveries, power outages, or the failure of the entire world black bean crop. You can't get away with being lazy for long. If you are, you get the reputation of being one of those flaky places that operates at the whim of some eccentric cook, who serves what she feels like when she feels like it. Maybe some people can live and survive that way, but I'm not one of them.

Naming Things

The first crucial naming decision was whether or not to change the name of the restaurant. When my sister and I were fantasizing, as teenagers, about owning a restaurant some day, we had what then seemed a terrific name all ready to go. The restaurant would specialize in salads, bread, and soup. I hereby give the name *Leaf, Loaf and Ladle* to the world. No royalties necessary.

Anyway, when we bought Cafe Beaujolais, we finally came to realize that that *was* its name. It just felt right. It's a nice name, I think, even if no one can spell it correctly. I get mail addressed to every possible variant, up to and including the Cafe Boogaloo. And when I telephone people and say, "I'm calling from Cafe Beaujolais," they'll

"On Sundays, the Beaujolais has a special brunch menu, which is all well and good, except it doesn't include some of the weekday greats. But you get saved because you can always go up to the Pig Out Window (the carry-out window) and say, 'Please can I have some country fries,' and Margaret will always make them for you."
—Regular Customer

say, "Hi, Cathy" (as in Cathy Boogaloo, I guess).

As for naming recipes, I tend to call them what they are, instead of something fanciful. In my 6:45 a.m. what-shall-I-make-today mode, I'm really not up for creative dish naming, anyway.

If I called my Sweet Pepper and Garlic Omelette (see page 184) an Omelette Scheherazade, for instance, the waiting staff would forever be answering the question, "What's in this Scheherazade?" Now they only spend part of that time answering the question, "What's in this Sweet Pepper and Garlic Omelette?" (The temptation to reply "prunes and nutmeg" is sometimes almost overwhelming.)

Often, the origins of names are lost in antiquity. I have no idea where Amazon Chocolate Cake (page 210) came from, but I really like that name. I thought up the name Silver Dollar French Toast for when we make it from baguettes. (I don't hear anyone laughing, but the intent was pure.) Once I made a cake which, upon being turned out of the pan, promptly broke into a thousand pieces. Needless to say, that was a time when I was making the dessert very close to the time it was going to be needed. There was absolutely no time to go back and make another. So I created a parfait with crumbled cake and pastry cream, and finished it off with whipped cream. It was perfectly delicious. No one had ever seen anything quite like it. I called it Gateau Brisé (or "broken cake"). We snickered in the kitchen.

Naming can be a marketing device, too. As I explain in the Fried Mush recipe (see page 196), when it appeared thus on the menu, we didn't sell very much. When I changed it to Fried Polenta, it took off.

The same situation prevails in writing menu copy. I don't go along with those restaurants where there is practically a sonnet accompanying every dish: "Carefully-selected extra-large ranch-fresh eggs from plump grain-fed chickens carefully blended with supermarket-fresh margarine and vine-ripened . . . " etc.

There has to be a proper balance. For us, that means a few adjectives along with the nouns, plus a well-informed waiting staff who can describe and answer questions about the various dishes. But it doesn't *always* work. My father is absolutely convinced that putting baked apples on the menu is my ticket to success. I've tried every way I can think of to get people to eat them (see page 218), but no matter how I describe them on the menu, no one orders them. My mom makes them with dried fruit and nuts and they're wonderful. Very sweet, but sweetness has never stopped people from ordering a dish. Still, something must have happened in the collective unconscious of the American public that has turned them off baked apples. I tell my father how many I've had to throw out, but he doesn't hear me.

What Goes on the Menu

There's no elaborate process at work here. It's my restaurant, and I must be the final arbiter. I'll try dishes out on friends whose tastes I really value, and of course I taste everything myself.

It's all highly personal. A lot of things on my breakfast menu are inspired by my father. He used to be on the road a lot. He'd come home and say, "You just can't get a good bowl of hot cereal any more." So now I always have two kinds of hot cereal on the menu—even when my father *isn't* visiting Mendocino.

It's a lot more tricky to figure out what *doesn't* go on the menu than what does. Sometimes I'm tempted to take something off because it is simply too popular. I'd love to be able to force people to try other things.

This is the case with Chicken Stuffed Under the Skin (page 150). I'm happy when things sell well, but it thwarts the spirit when you're offering six great dishes and people order just one. Taking that one away is, in a sense, training our customers to be more creative. But then we have to take the flak: "What do you mean you don't have that dish? I drove all the way from Los Angeles just to . . . ." Now at least I can say, "Buy this book and make your own."

"The only sad part about a one-day jaunt to Mendocino is that in a single visit to Margaret Fox's Cafe Beaujolais you can't manage to eat everything you'd like to eat.

Of course, if you started from home at daybreak, you could get to the Beaujolais in time for a late breakfast, then go for a long walk or explore Mendocino's quaint shops, and return for a late lunch. Better yet, plan a two-day trip. The restaurant is that good. What's more, prices are modest and portions are more than generous."

—Maggie Crum,
Food Editor
West County Times

There are some things not on the menu that I'd like to try if I could figure out how. Soufflés, for instance. I love them, and there are so many different kinds, from hors d'oeuvres through desserts. But you need a special oven, which means more space, and you can't have vibrations going on. We may need a separate Hall of Soufflés in an adjoining building.

Another frustration is the problem of dealing with dishes where the wonderful thing is in the presentation. For instance, there are elaborate ice cream desserts like bombes, but if a customer ordered a serving, they would get a slice, which wouldn't be nearly as nice for their aesthetic appreciation as seeing the whole thing. It's easier to make a fancy entrée for one or two than a fancy dessert for one or two.

Pricing and Portions

Where do prices come from? There really isn't a simple or clear-cut answer to this. Restaurant books for the most part give you the idea that there are handy formulas and charts you can use. Multiply the cost of the ingredients by X and you have your menu price.

But that's not really true. There are other factors operating. One is what the market will bear. There's a certain kind of negotiation that goes on between prices on the menu. For instance, if I have a piece of meat that costs a lot of money to buy, I won't mark it up to the same degree that I can mark up an egg. I'll mark the meat up less and the egg more.

Another factor is preparation time and energy. A steak doesn't take much time to fix, but there are things like roast peppers where we have to go through a laborious process: peeling them, marinating them and all. But we know that no one would spend more money for an hors d'oeuvre of grilled peppers than for a steak. Again, we have to even it out.

Then there's the ambience. If you like fresh flowers on your plate, if you like being cosseted, taken care of and crooned over by a waitress who has time to treat you right;

and if you want unsalted butter, pure maple syrup and no microwaves and on and on, you must realize that all of this costs money. It's not the same as a hash house where a gum-chewing waitress named Madge whirls the plate onto the counter and sashays off.

Price is, of course, closely tied to the size of portions. This is where things get very different from running a household, because I can't scrape my leftovers back into the pot. Restaurant books tell you to watch the leftovers closely as a clue to portion size and customer preference. That doesn't work for us, because by and large people eat all of whatever we give them. Once, due to a communication failure, we were briefly giving people triple-sized portions of fresh salmon. No one complained, and no one left any behind (or even asked for a doggie creel to take it home). They probably thought, "At last, a restaurant that serves enough food."

A good way to explain the importance of portion control is something a friend of mine overheard while sitting in the back of Mike's Pool Hall, which was then a very casual-seeming unstructured-looking San Francisco restaurant. An assistant asked the chef, "On the ravioli special, is it seventeen or eighteen raviolis?" Increasing the portion size by $1/17$th could easily spell the difference between profit and loss on that dish.

So we pay close attention to portions. We regularly re-weigh or remeasure the portions in the kitchen so we all know just what they should look like.

Our prices aren't low for Mendocino, but they are by city standards. That doesn't necessarily mean we'd be more profitable in the city, because all the operating costs would be higher, too. But the volume would be much greater. When I come down to San Francisco or Berkeley to eat, I'm just amazed at the volume. What would be a slow night in the city would be busy beyond our wildest expectations. Spenger's Fish Grotto in Berkeley often does more business in one *day* than we do in a *month*.

For us, a terrifically busy day would consist of serving between 250 and 300 customers during the day, and another 80 to 90 for dinner. It's nice to work at or near maximum occupancy. We all work better under those conditions. Our staff is responsible and concerned and committed, and it winds up being a tremendous burden on them to use their time creatively or effectively when business is slow. So, even though I wouldn't want to go beyond our present thirty-eight chairs, I'd like people in them all the time, please.

Everything ultimately comes down to the bottom line. My most important management data are the monthly profit and loss statements, which give me actual reflections on how much I am making or losing. I tend frequently to self-correct, in terms of repricing things. In the early days, I had a real concern about raising prices—cracking the $2 barrier on something that had been $1.95 for a long time. But when I did, most people didn't notice, and of the few who did, some chided me for not raising it sooner, because they had felt it was too low. (So why didn't they tell me earlier?)

This notion of underpricing is especially relevant with wines. These days I can buy good imported wine for around $40 a case, and using the rule of thumb that says to double it, I could sell it for $7 a bottle. But many people are suspicious of something too cheap. When I put it up to $8 or $9 a bottle it sells well. And the customers are still getting a good bargain, unlike the situation at some elegant-looking establishments that buy schlock wine really cheaply and mark it up astronomically. I don't know what's worse—the price gouging, or perpetrating that horror on someone's palate.

Reservations

As will become clear, this is a matter on which I am quite ambivalent, as are a good many other restaurant owners. When we first opened, we accepted reservations from anyone. But people were distressingly nonchalant about not showing up. One July 4th weekend, a party of sixteen called twenty minutes before they were supposed to arrive to say they weren't coming. It was too late to fill those seats—nearly half the restaurant—and it was horrible—the sort of thing that can completely ruin a small restaurant. It wasn't just the loss of revenues, but also the fact that we had purchased food for all those people.

Another time, something even more annoying happened. A woman who worked for me, but happened to be in another restaurant in town, overheard this guy come in and make a reservation for a party of six. She knew he had already made a reservation at the Cafe Beaujolais for the same time. We checked around and found a third restaurant was also involved.

Clearly this devil-may-care party was going to go where it felt like going, and to hell with the other two places. We three restaurants got together and cancelled *all* their reservations. It gave us a great feeling. Talk about vindictive! There is some justice left in the world. When the party of six did show up, they were appropriately shocked. But that kind of behavior is totally unacceptable, especially when you're dealing with very small and often financially precarious restaurants.

Everybody wants to say they've been to some charming little restaurant in the country, but there's a responsibility that goes both ways. Some customers have to be more conscious of that. It's not as if we flourish by dipping into some pot of gold whenever we need money. Our financial situation and business economy is just as real to us as it is to any other business that exists. Please remember that when you make reservations. End of sermon. Thank you.

Anyway, after this I decided not to take reservations at all. If people want to eat here, I said, they're going to have to tough it out. But then, after a while, I decided to take reservations for parties of five or more. Then I decided to take reservations for the evening meal. And I've *just* decided to take reservations for all parties at all times. I hope that now that we're better known, and people really want to come here, instead of selecting us randomly from the yellow pages, they're less likely to cancel. At least we'll give it a try for the coming season.

"When there was a five-person minimum for reservations, the two of us used to go out and recruit people on the sidewalk to get our minyan, as it were. 'You mean you haven't been to The Beauj?' we'd say. 'Can you come with us right now? You won't regret it.' "

—Local Couple

An interesting situation develops whenever a good review of us appears in a newspaper or magazine. There are people who seem to sit around waiting for reviews to come out, and then they rush off to those places the same day. When Stan Sesser's encomium on us appeared in the *San Francisco Chronicle*, the phone was ringing off the hook for days. It was wonderful. But then this doctor called and said he was making a reservation for a party of four for the next evening, a Saturday. I told him we were booked solid. He said, no, perhaps I didn't under*stand*. He and his guests were *very important people*, and he demanded a table. I informed him as sweetly as I could that we had only thirty-eight chairs, and every one of them was already reserved. He slammed down the phone. And I thought, what price fame. But happily that type of thing is very rare.

There are probably at least three Master's theses worth of sociology in what goes on at our big table, which can seat eight or ten. When things are crowded, we ask people if they'd be willing to share a table. Usually they agree. Some sit there staring stonily ahead as if there were walls between the chairs. Others are passing around photos of their grandchildren even before the freshly squeezed orange juice arrives. Some start out aloof, but by the time they leave, they've grown at least somewhat more interactive.

Our biggest group? People have reserved the whole restaurant on a number of occasions. Wedding or birthday parties, or just large groups of people. There's a motorcycle club that comes down from Eureka each year. No, not Hell's Angels. A very respectable middle-class group of very nice people.

Alcohol

We have a beer and wine license, which is no problem to get. Wine is important in my life, and it is unthinkable not to have it available with food (although, as it turns out, it's primarily the tourists, not the locals, who buy it).

In my fleeting fantasies, I think that I'd like to have a liquor license so I can serve after-dinner drinks. But those

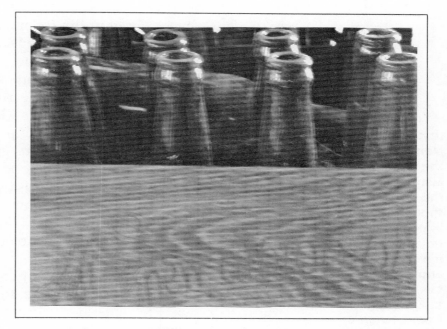

licenses are incredibly expensive, because there is a fixed number for the entire county, and whenever someone gives one up, it is auctioned off, usually for many tens of thousands of dollars.

An amusing sidelight here is the matter of using alcohol—liqueurs, brandy, bourbon, whatever—in cooking. State law now permits us to do this as long as the beverage itself has been rendered undrinkable by the addition of salt. The question then becomes precisely how much salt do we have to put into the Grand Marnier to satisfy the state inspector (and what an intriguing job he must have) and still keep it usable in cooking.

Thankfully there's no such problem with wines. My wine selections are made on a very personal basis. I go to wine tastings; I read newsletters; people bring wines to me; and I especially enjoy visiting the excellent wineries that abound in our part of the state. If I like it, I serve it; if I don't, I don't.

It seems essential, with the scope of our business, to keep the list small. During busy times, I will have about a dozen still (non-sparkling) wines on the list, and perhaps six to eight more on hold in the cellar. At any given time, we'll have 400 to 500 bottles on hand.

We offer some domestic and some foreign. I have no problem with the concept of all domestic—there are so many good wines coming from the nearby valleys of Mendocino, Sonoma, and Napa counties—but unfortunately the good domestics cannot keep up financially. The strength of the American dollar means good foreign wines are much less expensive now than good domestics.

Some of the smaller wineries release some limited special vintages just to restaurants. They give us a special marketing edge, which I appreciate. Navarro wines, from Philo, about twenty miles down the road from Mendocino, is one of my favorites.

Corkage is a big issue these days among restaurant owners. Should customers be permitted to bring their own wines? If so, what fee should be charged for opening and serving it to them? The range appears to be from a few dollars (we charge $3) up to $15 a bottle.

From a business standpoint, low-priced corkage isn't the wisest decision, since we *do* make money on the wine we sell. But I want people to enjoy wine with their meals, and if they prefer their own to mine, that's all right. Perhaps it's easy to say this, since it only happens once or twice a month. If it were a daily occurrence, I'd reserve the right to have second thoughts.

The Competition

There are perhaps half a dozen other restaurants in Mendocino (they come and they go), and we generally have a good relationship with them. When we're fully booked, we send people along to one of our competitors, and they do the same for us. During the winter, when our breakfast and lunch customers learn we're not doing dinner, they ask us for recommendations.

There's a mutual aid society in operation, too. People in town have loaned us water when our well went dry or the pump broke down, and those are real friends. Only people who live in places where they're dependent on their own

"I started my restaurant in Mendocino right at the same time Margaret took over the Beaujolais. Even though we were living in the same house, we almost never saw one another—but we'd talk on the telephone a lot from kitchen to kitchen. 'How many dinners did you serve tonight? We found a good supplier for croissants. There's a tour bus in town. We tossed out a belligerent drunk and I fear he's heading your way.' That sort of thing."
—Former Competitor

wells can appreciate how important that i...

This kind of interaction—borrowing suga... gredients back and forth—is fairly common... towns. I've heard from people in other parts of the... that Northern California is especially known for ... maraderie of its restaurant owners.

In one sense, that's the only sensible way to live. Ex-treme or intense competition takes up a tremendous amount of time and energy. And yet it's really curious when you think about it. Every couple that eats elsewhere in town has, in effect, taken $20 or $30 out of my pocket.

But being in business is a gamble—a gamble I am, of course, willing to take. I gamble that enough people will come in for me to run a viable restaurant. And also (can I say this without offense?) I've got to believe that once people eat at Cafe Beaujolais, they'll elect to return here. Of course that's what the people who run our competition think about *their* places too, and that's fine. There's room enough in this town for all of us.

I'm always interested in what the competition is doing. When a Burger King and a big new coffee shop went in about ten miles up the highway, I somehow felt they wouldn't have any noticeable effect on our business, and I was right. But events like that remind me that I must always be on my toes, so to speak. Not that I would say I'm 100% complacent, but there are always important is-sues to attend to, and if the freezer motor is making funny noises and the chocolate shipment is late, it's easy not to spend a lot of time thinking about the competition.

The Garden

When we first started the restaurant, we had every inten-tion of running a full-scale garden that would supply most of the vegetables for the kitchen. The fantasy, and I guess it's quite a common one among would-be restaurant start-ers, was that we could just step outside the kitchen door and pluck the lettuces or carrots or beans or tomatoes or peas from the garden, and rush them onto the table.

We had full-time gardeners, and spent a good deal of money trying to get it together, but sadly it proved to be economically unfeasible. We could do it up to a certain point, but that kind of gardening is really too labor-intensive to be practical.

So now we use the acre of land surrounding the restaurant—for growing a tremendous amount of flowers, and also herbs. (We grow edible flowers, like nasturtiums and chive blossoms—little purple balls that taste like chives—and borage flowers, which are beautiful intense periwinkle blue flowers that taste like cucumbers. When the waitresses tell the customers that they can eat the flowers on their plates, people go, "Oh, don't be silly," but if they try it, they usually love it.)

The two main reasons we still spend a lot of time and effort on the garden are that it looks great, and that I need it psychologically for my own benefit. The fact that it pleases the customers so much happens to be a great side benefit. But I would keep the garden going for myself, no matter what.

For years, I had a running argument with my accountant over how costly the garden was. I decided that I didn't care about that, because when you work as hard as you have to work at running a restaurant, by golly you'd better get a lot of pleasure out of *some*thing.

It's always been wonderful to be able to go out into the garden and see all the different flowers, the hummingbirds, the garden snakes, and the butterflies. There are times when I think it kept me from going completely bonkers.

The customers love it too. It has an old-fashioned feeling. Very much cared for, and yet not overdone. Josh Shook and Desiree Douglass, our gardeners, work hard at that. They don't run around clipping every single blade of grass so that they're all the same height. Things have a sort of wild and laid back sprawling look. The Blanche DuBois of the gardening world, you might say. (My mother says that Mendocino is the only place in the world where even the weeds look great; that she has the same weeds in her garden and they look like weeds instead of something you want to make a line drawing of.)

The Kitchen

Many of the customers who come back to look at our kitchen tell me that they've had the dream of installing a commercial or restaurant kitchen in their home. Then they look around, and are often surprised to see that what we have really isn't so different from what they left behind in suburbia.

Ours is a fairly small kitchen. The building was built in the early 1900s, which was not a time of super-efficient high-tech space usage. The day we moved in, we gutted the kitchen. We rebuilt the shelves and cupboards, and then acquired a small amount of machinery.

The few pieces of equipment we have are larger than you'd find in most homes—the stove, the dishwasher, the mixer, the food processor, the espresso machine—but they're not any different in function. If there's an automatic electronic omelette flipper out there, it has not come to my attention.

The things that make our kitchen different from many restaurant kitchens (in addition to the quality of food com-

ing out of it!) are the things we don't have. We *don't* have fluorescent lights, because I hate them. (They were here when I bought the building, but we took them out promptly.)

We don't have microwave ovens, and that's both a cooking statement and a health statement and an everything else statement. Once, when I was employed as a baker at the Mendocino Hotel, I put a croissant in their microwave to heat it. Perhaps the setting was wrong, but in any event, before my very eyes, that lovely croissant turned inside out. The entire butter content of the dough was exuded into a greasy pool, and what had been, in its former lifetime, a perfectly respectable croissant melted into a gummy mess. There and then, I said to myself that anything that can do that to a croissant will never be used by my hands. We will *never* have microwaves in our kitchen.

One thing we do have that's unusual, surprisingly enough, is windows. Our windows look out on lovely things, like the ocean and the garden. Many professional kitchens don't have windows. It is supposed to be more efficient without them, I guess, but the combination of the windows, the light paint on the walls, and the high ceiling, makes our kitchen a pleasant place, with a nice country feel to it.

Of course it's too small, which is the familiar chorus you hear in almost all restaurant kitchens. We've thought about the possibility of expanding our kitchen, but that would require $20,000 to $30,000, and I don't think it will happen in the forseeable future.

However, in our first seven years, we've reinvested some of the revenues to make slow and modest progress in the way of physical changes. New wallpaper. A satisfactory cash register. A little espresso room off the dining room. We took out one wall that divided the dining room (which seemed to upset half our regular customers and please the other half). Things like that.

In the months or years to come, we'll continue adding modestly to our array of equipment, but nothing world-shattering. We could use a larger mixer because twenty quarts just isn't big enough any more. But that's about it for now. We're unlikely to get a restaurant management computer, for instance. My wish list doesn't include those multitudes of wonders depicted in full color in the restaurant management magazines each month.

Suppliers

It would be so easy if everything came from the same source. For some restaurants, of course, it does. The truck from the wholesaler backs up to the door once a week and unloads everything from the curry powder to the portion-controlled flash-frozen ready-to-microwave entrées.

For us, there is a continuing search for new suppliers— a search that I love. Some are right here in Mendocino. The staples do come up on that truck from the city. Standard produce comes from standard produce suppliers. But when we want something esoteric, such as mangoes or radicchio, we go without until we can figure out how to get it from the city.

There's a rule of thumb, I guess. Even if you want to operate a rural restaurant, try to pick a location that is no more than one day's round-trip drive from a big city. Many times, we'll have to go or send someone down to San Francisco or Berkeley to pick up rare produce or other unusual ingredients. Monterey Foods in Berkeley is probably one of the best produce sources in creation. Sometimes their special restaurant prices on ordinary items, like asparagus, are less than our wholesalers' prices. It actually pays us to drive those 150 miles and buy things there.

Whenever possible, of course, we prefer to deal with local suppliers, and with friends—and the two are often synonomous.

Even though I am extremely supportive of people who go into business for themselves with quality food products, there's no point in going into rhapsodies over things that simply cannot be bought outside of a limited geographical area. Fortunately, through the magic of mail order, the number of such items is growing ever smaller.

That's why this book includes the section on page 256, in which I describe many of the good food products I use that *can* be bought by mail (or, in many cases, locally if you approach the manager of a good local food store.)

The story of our coffee is typical of the blend of product, personality, and other factors that go into our buying decisions. Paul and Joan Katzeff have their own little coffee factory—Thanksgiving Coffee—about ten miles north of us at Noyo Harbor. When we were starting out, I thought about this, but felt that I would get better consistency and quality from big city suppliers.

But I kept hearing good things about Thanksgiving Coffee. Then a friend and I went to a coffee tasting with the Katzeff's, and sipped for about 3½ hours. It was a revelation. I learned that coffees are as complex as chocolates and wines. I was impressed, and I wound up buying all my coffee from Thanksgiving. We developed our own blend, which is sold both in stores and by mail as Cafe Beaujolais House Blend.

The psychologist in me is fascinated by the phenomenon of the entrepreneur, and the form that entrepreneurial interest takes. The interest range is often limited to one product done well. Paul and Joan will never get into condiments. Devora Rossman, who makes the very special hot-and-sweet-and-sour-all-at-once Mendocino Mustard we use and sell will never get into cheeses. Laura Chenel became so involved with goat cheese, she not only has her own little factory, she wrote a wonderful book on the subject (*Chèvre: the Goat Cheese Cookbook*; Aris Books, Berkeley).

It's hard for me to imagine getting into goat cheese or caramels or chocolate chips or herbs for even two days. Yet somehow these other people were captivated in the same way I was captivated by my restaurant (and by our Panforte di Mendocino and other products we make and sell by mail).

Finally, a few words on produce and spices.

Produce: The importance of fresh, quality produce should not be underestimated. Although we do buy as much as we can locally, it has never worked out to have people growing things on commission for us. We were at the mercy of the vagaries of weather, soil, and individual behaviors. Still, when people approach me, as they regularly do, I get really extravagant. "Bring me all the tomatoes you can. Bring me all the basil you can." It's not as if they have 100 acres and this 18-wheeler full of basil is going to back up to the door. Sometimes we do get a little overwhelmed, especially by apples in the fall, but that's OK.

Spices: Fresh spices are so very important, and supermarket spices are never fresh. Yes, I know life would go on with boxed, powdered ginger instead of freshly grated ginger, but it wouldn't go on as well. Many herbs and spices can be grown in a kitchen garden, and again, we have our urban suppliers half a day away. But in most cases, I'd rather not make something at all than make it with dried, powdered, stale supermarket blends.

Problems

No one ever said running a restaurant was easy. As a convenience to people who (a) want to know what they may be in for if they start a restaurant, (b) would rather read about other people's troubles than contemplate their own, or (c) collect stories of maple syrup disasters, I've assembled all the negative or difficult or troublesome things I have to say into this one section, neatly subdivided. The order is quite random; it's hard to imagine how it could be otherwise.

Bad checks: A very minor problem for us. We never get more than one or two a month, usually for small amounts. The majority are from local people who usually make good on them. Even the out-of-town ones usually turn out to be a sincere error of some sort, although there was that quite large one from a Utah couple whose names I am tempted to include at this point in bold face type.

Bad credit cards: Again, a minor problem, but not quite as minor as bad checks. Most of the problems were, in a sense, our own fault because either we didn't bother to phone in for authorization if the card limit was exceeded or we ignored our own suspicions. We're a lot more careful than we used to be.

Dying customers: It's never happened, but we *are* trained in first aid, and all of the staff have learned how to apply the Heimlich Maneuver to people who are choking. Thankfully, we've never needed to use it.

Walkouts: In our first seven years, only a dozen or so people have walked out without paying. It's a small number, but I remember them all quite vividly. I fervently hope they will end up incarcerated for other crimes they may perpetrate against the well-meaning.

Babies, having: None has been born on the premises, but we do seem to have the peculiar reputation as a place that pregnant women go to when they want to go into labor. Some who are a little overdue have even been sent here by their friends or family.

Babies, wailing: I'm never quite sure how to deal with this problem, but I fear we don't do too well. The entire dining room is tense, thinking, "Why won't this kid shut up." More often than not, the parents are sitting there smiling, completely unperturbed. Don't they hear it? Or do they think every utterance of their precious darling is just fabulous?

There have been times when the waiting staff suggests that a parent might like to take the child for a little walk around the garden. That's more socially acceptable than what I'd like to do, which is put my hand over their mouth and yank them right out the door.

For slightly older children, we do have a little basket of toys we bring over for them to play with.

Babies, nursing: Some restaurants get really uptight about this, I know, but I'm not sure anyone has ever complained, and it's fine with me.

Smoking: I can't stand smoking myself, but I do allow cigarettes (no cigars) because I think it would cause a lot of repercussions if I didn't. Some of my best friends, alas, are smokers. I think it's a horrible habit, and I never willingly eat next to someone who is smoking.

We do have a separate smoking area, but it's still a very small dining room. The waiting staff is very good about juggling people around, and the customers rarely complain. If they ask to be moved, then of course we do it.

Thankfully, fewer and fewer people are smoking in the restaurant these days. They tend to cluster at a table in one corner. We've thought about installing a trap door.

Complaints: They do happen occasionally. Nearly all of the complaints are about minor things that can be handled on the spot: warming the soup, changing a vegetable, re-adding the bill, whatever. Once in a while, people write letters of complaint. The portions were too small (or too large!) for them. We didn't have the specials some review had mentioned. Only a handful every year. I always answer them politely, even when they are unfair, as in the case of the man who complained bitterly because, when he and his party arrived shortly after our closing time, we didn't let them in. If we'd had food left, we probably would have admitted them anyway, but it had been busy and exhausting day and the cupboards were bare. He got a polite letter too.

Lingerers: Most of the time, we're delighted when people sit around and talk and relax and think of us as their second home. But when the restaurant is crowded, with a lot of people waiting, and a party has been at a table for a long time after finishing their meal, we do try to encourage them to depart. We bring them their bill, and ask if there's anything more we can get for them, perhaps they'd like to take their coffee with them in a "to go" cup. I hate to ask people bluntly to leave, but eventually it is done. People are almost always great about it; we've never had any trouble.

Language problems: A fair number of foreign visitors come through Mendocino, and many of them end up at the Beaujolais. Most parties will have at least one member who speaks English, but if not, we always manage to get along. No one flies directly from Tokyo to Mendocino International. By the time people get here, they're already quite adept at pointing to things, and using gestures and smiles to get what they want. And I am always standing by, ready to use my French when it is called for.

Customer theft: We lose a small amount of salt and pepper shakers and tableware, but it has never been enough of a problem to install metal detectors and one-way mirrors.

Teenagers: It seems a cyclical sort of thing. There have been times when we've had a problem with large numbers of teenagers hanging out in the restaurant during school hours. An order of country fries for six people. In recent months, it hasn't been a problem at all. Where do they go instead? To school? That would be novel.

Unruly customers: It's a rare problem, but when it does occur, we're always nervous about how to deal with it. We don't want to rock the boat, even when the customer is already rocking the boat. The waitresses are really very good at handling those people, and I strongly encourage them to do so. I don't want to be held up as "Mommy in the kitchen, who will have to come out and deal with you."

Unusual customers: Mendocino has its share of eccentrics, bizarre-looking or dressing or acting people, and even a few genuine loonies. At one time or another, they do come in to the restaurant, and of course we serve them. There have been times when a couple has come up from Marin County in their Mercedes for some very special holiday, and they come to Cafe Beaujolais because they've

"I appreciate the fact that the first amendment, or whatever it is, guarantees the right of assembly, but I must say that some of the people who assemble here make my wife and me feel distinctly uncomfortable. We try to get to Mendo twice a year, and this place has the best food, but I wish they'd consider a dress code, like Heritage House."
—Tourist

heard so much about it, and in comes someone they'd cross three streets to avoid back home and he's seated next to them and treated in the same way as they. It does make for some difficult moments sometimes, but we all survive.

I remember the young man who used to have breakfast with Albert Einstein. He would come in for breakfast carrying a huge box, and he'd take a corner seat facing out into the dining room. He'd remove a large bronze bust of Einstein and set it on the table while he ate. That lasted for about a week. Nobody batted an eye. Everything's relative, I guess.

Misguided cooks: We employ a fair number of local people who don't necessarily have professional restaurant training. Most of the time, there are no problems with this, but there have been a few.

We were in the midst of a typically frantic dinner preparation time, and the dinner cook asked a young man to strain the chicken stock—the very vital fluid that we were needing for several sauces. So Jim went over to the sink, and very diligently poured all the stock down the drain and kept the bones.

In the same vein, as it were, we once had a cook who, it turned out, was using our best cellar wines in lavish quantities to make soup. We would have had to charge $20 for a bowl of that soup.

Staff theft: I may be extremely naive, since industry averages are rather alarming in this regard, but I would say that we do not have any premeditated staff theft. I would be very surprised if it were happening—but if anyone ever *did* get caught, he or she would be fired on the spot. I try to be fair, but that one I couldn't take.

Food spills: We haven't had any gigantic food-dropping disasters worthy of a Chaplin film, possibly because our waiting staff doesn't use trays. Once a customer gestured wildly as four large drinks were passing by him, and we had Fantasias propelled all over the dining room. And Janet has had the odd bagel Frisbee itself off a plate—once di-

rectly into someone's coffee (but fortunately it was someone we knew).

And then there was the Great Maple Syrup Caper. We
store five-gallon cans of syrup upstairs, and transfer it into
one-liter bottles for use in the kitchen. One time, Janet was
in a hurry, so she set the big can dripping slowly into the
smaller bottle and went about her business. An hour and
a half later, she remembered, rushed upstairs, and sure
enough, there was syrup all over the floor. She mopped it
up, and thought that was the end of it.

But no. An immense amount had seeped through the
cracks in the floor, and for about ten days, it kept dripping
through the dining room ceiling. We hung little Chinese
take-out cartons on the ceiling to catch it, and called it
our shrine to Aunt Jemima.

Accidents: We've had our share of breaking out the first
aid kit or rushing someone up to the emergency room at
Coast Hospital, but this is a book about restaurants, not
medicine, so I shall not go into any gruesome details. Most
particularly, I will not discuss the car antenna incident.

Theft: We did have one break-in, but all the person stole
was some coffee cake (see page 190). The thief came in
through the rather tiny bathroom window, and there were
crumbs all over the roof.

The only big robbery was an inside job. It was in August
of 1979, before we had learned enough to bank our money
through the night depository every night. I had hired a
temporary dishwasher. He seemed really dumb, but he was
smart enough to figure out where we hid the money. He
stole $1,500, and even worse was the feeling of how he
had violated the premises. I didn't even want to be in the
building for days, I felt so rotten. It was as if there was this
lingering presence of a horrible person.

Staff disobedience: Everyone is really good about following instructions and maintaining our standards. The only
serious insurrection is over the matter of pineapple in our
granola (see page 201). The serving staff started adding it

"I remember
when Margaret got
one of her first
huge special orders
for a whole bunch
of Queen Mother
cakes—very
wonderful chocolate
cakes. She had
divided scads of
egg yolks and
whites, and while
she was off on the
phone, somehow
the cake ingredients
all fell into the
brown sauce for the
evening's dinner,
thus ruining both.
She came marching
into my kitchen, sat
on the counter, and
said, 'Just cook.
Don't talk. I just
want to watch for a
while.' And then she
went back and
pulled everything
together. She did
great."
—Former Competitor

on their own, and even though I think it's a bit odd that way, the staff loves it, and the public isn't complaining, so I let it go by. If they started putting anchovies in the granola, I'd put my foot down, however.

The weather: One of the problems of serving food outdoors, of course, is that we are at the mercy of the gods. Normally we study the forecasts and the heavens and all goes well, but there have been a few occasions when the skies opened up on a deck full of diners, even a Sunday morning or two when the place was jammed. But the customers are always very understanding—they're quite sure it wasn't my fault, and they just stand around with their plates full of water until tables open up inside.

No water: There have been times when we have run completely out of water. The well's gone dry or our pump is broken, and we don't know it until our storage tank is completely empty. City people find this very hard to understand. "What do you *mean* I can't have oatmeal because there's no water. How can there be no water?" Eventually we find a plumber and he fixes the pump, or we find the man with the tank truck to bring us some water, and in the meantime we borrow water from one of our neighbors.

No electricity: This is a fairly common occurrence in the area, especially when storms hit the coast or tourists hit the power poles. Our stove works on propane, so we light the candles and keep on going. We can't do waffles or coffee, but at least we can stay open. It may be charming and cozy out front, but it's no fun trying to run a kitchen by candlelight.

Exploding espresso machine: This is one of my mother's major fears in life. If you don't tighten everything down, it might blow up. Has it ever happened to us? Since my mom is going to be reading this book, I have nothing more to say on the subject, except to remind people always to tighten everything down on their espresso machines and treat them with respect.

THE CUSTOMERS

The Tourists and the Locals

I'm glad we have a balance between them. Actually there are three categories of customers: the locals, tourists who have been coming here regularly for years, and those who are here for the first time. As a rough guess, I'd said it's about 40:40:20 in those three categories, but of course the ratios are quite seasonal. There are a lot more locals in the winter months.

We can relax a little more with the locals, and that's positive—but then the tourists are more likely to spend more, to have wine and so forth, and we like that, too. The locals rarely order wine. They come in before or during work, so they're less likely to drink during the day.

Surprisingly, the tourists don't necessarily tip better. Our locals tip very well, especially considering that this is not a wealthy town. Then again, it's actually harder to wait on the locals sometimes. They seem to expect more. Perhaps it's that they come in so often, we have a tendency to take them for granted. There are people who come in every day of the week and have for years.

In fact, when I'm in the kitchen cooking and certain orders come in, I know precisely who it is out there. When I see a ticket for "one scram, half fries," I know that Tom is here. If its "eggs cooked hard" (which I think of as "eggs, ruined") then it's Gene Parsons.

Those of our waiting staff who have worked elsewhere tell me that one difference here is that we *do* often know the customers' names. Other places, customers are known only as the Special Breakfast #2 man, or the Two Eggs Over, Hold the Potatoes, Ketchup Please lady. Such a way to go through life!

I Am a Hu-Man Be-Ing

There are times when the Elephant Man's plaintive lament comes to mind. When people are here on vacation, they sometimes tend to forget that we who live here are real people, too. A tourist was waiting to use the phone while a staff member was talking to the school about some prob-

> "At the end of the summer, when we've been dealing with the tourists for months, one of the real joys of my life is to book a table at the Beaujolais on a Saturday evening. Then we come to town, looking like locals. There's this long line outside, but we just waltz past them all. They're giving us these *looks*."
>
> —Local Resident

lem. You could just see the realization slowly sink in, that we are not just munchkins here to bring them breakfast. We are just like them. We make our beds and pay the rent and have a real existence. Neither the waiting staff nor I are happy with the pat-on-the-head patronizing attitude that a few tourists bring. We do try to remember that feeling when we're traveling and being tourists in other people's villages or cities.

And yet we're well aware that it's quite a different game dealing with tourists. They are here for a vacation, for a good time. We really want to make it a special experience for them—to convey to them that everything is under control, and we really have it together; that we're proud of what we're able to do for them.

There's an interesting sociology at work here. Because many people come to Mendocino for a week or so, and there just aren't that many places to eat, we will see the same people intensively. We really become a part of each others' lives for those few days, and then, in most cases never see each other again. We develop a rapport that's an unusual blend of closeness and keeping our distance.

I'm not the kind of owner who enjoys making an appearance in the dining room on regular intervals, shaking hands at every table, saying "Hi, I'm the owner. Hope you're enjoying the meal." Even though I think that's perfectly fine and even lovely and gracious for others to do, I get a little embarrassed, and prefer it when people come into the kitchen to visit me.

And they do. Customers often ask to see the kitchen (we are glad to oblige), and to meet the cook. I remember when I was little, going by restaurant kitchens and thinking, "Wow, it seems like such a different world in there." Even now, looking in from the outside, the lights are brighter, and there's din and bustle, and hard work going on. So yes, please come and visit the kitchen, but please don't expect to stand there and chat for half an hour. It may look easy, but we really are concentrating on what we're doing with all the brain cells we've got.

"There are times when I feel almost hostile when I see a line of these strangers outside my Beaujolais on a Sunday morning. They've driven up from the Bay Area in their BMW's, wearing their brand new L.L. Bean boots and the adventurous ones wear their Buck knives. They sort of look down their noses at me, but I have the inner satisfaction of knowing this is my restaurant, and my Cafe Beaujolais bill is somewhat higher than my mortgage. This place is good to locals."

—Local Resident

On the way to the restrooms, you have to pass the usu-ally-open door to the kitchen. People stick their heads in to say thank you. That makes me feel good—and so do the times when I see people taking photographs of their food. Still life with blueberry muffin.

Just as some tourists forget that they are dealing with real people, we on the staff must take care to remember that there are people out there eating this food we're work-ing so hard to prepare. Sometimes it leaves the door and we don't think about it any more.

Attire

We don't have a dress code, other than the state law against bare feet in a restaurant. Very few restaurants within 100 miles of here require neckties. We *will* serve gentlemen in ties, however. People do call up and ask what our dress code is, and we're always amused. We're just glad when they *wear* clothes. We tell people to wear whatever they feel comfortable in. It's all quite casual. We'll have people all dressed up sitting alongside others in jeans and T-shirts. That's fine with me, and I think almost all the customers feel comfortable with this too.

Celebrities

Some well-known people have come in, but for the most part we don't pay close attention. If Frank Sinatra swept in with his entourage, we'd certainly take notice, but if a celebrity gets to Mendocino, it either means they're work-ing here (as when movies are being filmed; when they were working on *Racing with the Moon* last year, Richard Ben-jamin, Elizabeth McGovern and Sean Penn ate here, for instance); or they're on holiday and probably are looking for a slice of normal life. They don't want to sign auto-graphs or be lionized.

We found out after the fact that a famous teen idol— Shaun Cassidy, I think—was in Mendocino on his honey-moon. Ted Koppel has been here, and Robert Redford, Johnny Carson, Bonnie Raitt, and some of the cast of *Same*

Time Next Year. Possibly Truman Capote and Ed Meese (albeit not together). For some reason, the customers once got all excited over a lady who's in a paper towel commercial. Such is fame.

I was thrilled when Julia Child came to visit. We had some terrific specials on the menu that day, but she ordered our old standby Black Bean Chili (see page 144). Now, when someone asks, "How's the chili?" there's a great temptation to say, "Well that's what Julia Child orders when *she* eats here."

The Doug Chouteau Section

I was going to put in a few anecdotes about unusual or amusing or peculiar things that have occurred with regard to our regular customers, and when I made a list, I realized that almost every one of them dealt with just one person, Doug Chouteau. So here's a small Doug Chouteau section.

Doug used to come into the restaurant every single day. He doesn't eat a lot. He'd arrive early with his *Wall Street Journal*, have a latté or a light breakfast, and spend hours and hours. He always wanted something different from whatever was on the menu. One sausage instead of three. Half a muffin. One egg cooked just so. It became something of a joke, but I really liked him, so I was willing to put up with this.

One day we had a special breakfast that wasn't particularly large, but naturally he wanted only half of it. So what I did was break a plate in half, with jagged edges, and I fixed up the plate as if it had been broken with the food already on it: two-thirds of a sausage, part of a scrambled egg, half a garnish, a partial orange slice. Boy, did that shut him up for a while.

Another time, he seemed to be suffering from terminal ambivalence. He kept discussing one alternative after another with his waitress, who had quite a few other people to wait on and was growing more and more exasperated. Finally she put her hands on her hips and said, "You know, it's not your *mother* cooking back there." He was quite taken aback. I think he had honestly forgotten he was in a restaurant.

Once he spent about ten minutes describing to his waitress precisely what ingredients he wanted in a special omelette, and how much of each, and exactly how it was to be cooked. I went out with one of our big big bowls with all the ingredients in it: the uncooked eggs, the fresh zucchini, the pan, the whisk, the whole thing, and said, "Look, you know what you want; you make it."

I don't think I'd want to have too many customers like Doug, but I do enjoy our relationship.

THE STAFF

One of the hardest things I had to learn was how to be a manager and a boss and a personnel officer and feel good about myself all at the same time. But in general it's all worked well, and I feel we have a remarkable staff now. In fact, from talking with many other people in the restaurant business, I conclude we may have the most responsible staff anyone has heard of.

That's what it's really all about: competence and responsibility. People literally *never* fail to show up here without letting us know in time for us to call someone else. Another important thing is that everybody can fill more than one role, if necessary. The waiting staff can bus tables and make drinks and act as cashier and do prepping. The busser can wash dishes. The prep cook can cook and wash and bus. And so it goes.

In fact, the only thing that must never happen at Cafe Beaujolais is for the owner to act as a waitress. After months of saying I'd be an awful one; I'm not cut out to be one; I don't *want* to be one—we were so busy that I actually *had* to be one. I was pouring coffee into somebody's cup, and, exactly as I had predicted, the coffee shot out the other side of the cup. It seemed as if about thirty gallons had been spilled on the customer, the table, the food, everything. I haven't waited on tables since then. It is not my métier.

The number of people on the floor depends entirely on how busy we are. The usual minimum, includes a cook, a prep cook, and a dishwasher in the kitchen, and two waiting staff in front. When the deck is open, we add a third. The other functions, (which sometimes have separate individuals filling them), are host or hostess, cashier, espresso machine operator, busser, plus, of course, part-time gardeners and our janitor.

On busy days, it's a pleasure to watch the restaurant in action. It's like a complicated ballet, with everybody moving quickly back and forth, and it all clicks. It's actually harder when things are slow and each person takes on more jobs. When you are cleaning or organizing your station in between customers, it's hard to get back into the pace or social mode required for the dining room.

"The people who work the longest at the Beaujolais are the ones who are extremely competent and who know how to, for lack of a better word, comfort Margaret. She does start growing anxious when she has umpty-ump things to do. If you can get your work done and maintain a kind of solidity in the kitchen, you can have your job there for a long, long time."

—Former Employee

Pooling

One thing we do which is quite unusual in restaurants is complete sharing of everything among the waiting staff. They pool customers, and they pool orders to pick up, instead of each person having his or her own territory and perish the thought that someone else should enter it.

The whole dining room and kitchen become a totality, and everyone in it does whatever has to be done to make it all run smoothly. We have a level of cooperation you don't see too often, and it really works well.

Hiring

Even with a relatively small staff, very low turnover, and in an area of pretty high unemployment, hiring has been a problem for us. There's a real shortage of well-trained, qualified people. A common fallacy in some job seekers' thinking is: "I like to cook; I can work in a restaurant;" or "I need money; I'll be a waitress."

Occasionally, however, the gods smile on us. A dishwasher quit suddenly, and we had to come up with a replacement instantaneously. One of the features of our rural life is a "classified ads" program on the radio every morning, in which people call in to sell their goats or look for a left rear fender for their pick-up truck. So we telephoned the program with our "help wanted" need, and lo and behold, a man appeared within five minutes, and he turned out to be just great. That's not the kind of thing I want to count on, but it's nice when it happens.

Training

Even though the people we hire have had restaurant experience elsewhere, we still do rather extensive training, because they don't have Cafe Beaujolais experience. I know what I want to convey—the atmosphere of graciousness, without being formal or stuffy: an environment where everyone feels comfortable. That's my goal, and my manager has taken on the responsibility for seeing that it happens. We all talk about problem situations and questions that arise, and somehow these things get reinterpreted into the job description. This usually works well, but there was that one young lady who couldn't understand why I didn't want "happy faces" put on the cottage cheese scoops. "They loved it at the last place I worked," she said.

The only continuing problem I have in training is to get the waiting staff to taste the specials. I introduce specials to them, and they say, "Uh huh, yes," and then sometime later they'll actually *taste* it and suddenly realize that it really *is* good, and *then* they go out and *really* sell it. I get a little annoyed when this happens. I say, "Do you think I lied to you when I said it was great? Trust me."

I like the staff to look neat and tidy and well-groomed at all times, and they always do. These days, they wear aprons with the Beaujolais bird on them.

Service

Service happens to be my big nudge. I want it to be absolutely perfect. Since it is so good already, I recognize that, as the owner, I may be a little unreasonable in demanding perfection.

The waiting staff is kind and friendly and helpful in a genuine way. I don't enjoy places where the waitress says, "Hi, my name is Rita, and I'll be your waitress this evening. I'm a Taurus with Scorpio rising, and I'd like to describe my specials."

Our staff has discovered that if you happen to give your name to certain kinds of customers, they will proceed to sit there and call, in an increasingly louder voice, "Judy! JUDY! I NEED YOU, JUDY!" And Judy has thirty-seven other people to deal with, so will he please quiet down over there.

Irritations

While the majority of our customers, locals and tourists, are wonderful people, we do have ones that drive the staff to distraction and back again. They want their order five minutes ago. They have quite unrealistic expectations.

"If I can't decide, I might say, 'I'd like something light but with protein'. And the waitress says, 'How about a scrambled egg, but I'll put some cheese on top.' It's a little thing, but it makes me feel important; that I'm cared about. I don't know what they say about me in the kitchen, but it always appears as if they really *enjoy* doing that kind of thing."
—Regular Customer

At the risk of sounding ridiculous and simplistic, I ask you to remember all those things your parents told you about working and playing well with others. You have to respect the fact that other people preceded you into the restaurant, and you've got to wait your turn. It's just not cool to snap your fingers and whistle at the waitress and say, "Miss, Miss, *Miss*." Our waitresses make few mistakes, and they work as hard and as fast as they can. Don't forget that they are people too.

Tipping

I think most people now realize that waitresses' wages are quite low because of the expectation of tips. Tips are generally in the area of 10% to 15% for breakfast, 15% to 20% for dinner, and somewhere in between for lunch. When local people don't leave a tip, it's usually because they don't have the money with them, but they'll leave more the next time they're in.

Once in a while, tourists who got excellent food and service leave without tipping. They probably think they'll never eat here again, so why not save a few dollars. That is, of course, their prerogative. It never even enters our minds to follow them back to their bed-and-breakfasts and let the air out of their tires.

PERSONAL MATTERS

Margaret Fox shows an early interest in food preparation.

Restaurant Critics

I've always been treated well by critics, so I have no axe to grind. And yet it seems to me that the whole food industry is becoming more and more of an in-group situation. It is growing harder for critics to draw the line between personal friendship interests or business interests on the one hand, and objectivity on the other.

The critic's role *should* be one of objectivity—or at least they must admit their subjectivity. If they don't do that, then I wonder if a so-called "critic's view" is any more valid or useful or important than anyone else's.

There is always the issue of anonymity. Some critics make a major issue of the fact that no one knows who they are, so they can be assured of not getting any special treatment. (I don't know if this is true, but I once read that half the restaurants in New York had pictures of Mimi Sheraton hanging in the kitchen when she was the influential restaurant critic for the *New York Times*.) Sometimes I know when a restaurant critic is eating at Cafe Beaujolais, and sometimes I don't. But I can honestly say that it doesn't matter, because he or she would get exactly the same food and service as anyone else, which is the only way it should be. If you serve good food, then you serve good food to everybody, including critics.

The power of critics can be considerable. We've gotten some fabulous reviews in various newspapers and magazines, and there's nothing like it. When the *San Francisco Chronicle* said many kind words, we started seeing people for lunch that very day—people who had made the 3½ hour trip after putting down their morning paper.

The impact of most reviews seems to last for about four or five weeks, during which time I think, "Oh, this is just great. If only our level of busy-ness remains this high." But it never does. It begins to taper off, and a few months later a customer may say, "Yeah, I think I read a review somewhere . . . ." Nonetheless, I'm convinced that each review helps to build the basic audience base for the restaurant, even if most of those people come in only once every year or two.

Eating Out

This is not a restaurant guide, in part because of space limitations, and in larger part because I simply have not been to many restaurants outside of California. (At this time, I do not fly. That is a bugaboo I must get over. I had thought that when I had all four wisdom teeth removed in one sitting, that was the ultimate in confronting problems and fear. But that was something I'll never have to do again. The problem with flying is that you have to get home. I wonder what would happen if I finally got to Europe and then decided I couldn't fly back. I'd be stuck there for the rest of my life. It could be worse, I guess.)

I do eat out a lot in Northern California, and I enjoy it. I'm very much aware of what I am eating (the culinary equivalent of a pilot flying on a commercial flight as a passenger, I imagine). So I pick the places I go to very carefully. I become quite an angry restaurant-goer if I get the feeling a place doesn't care, or if they think what they're doing is hot stuff and I don't.

But when I have a good experience, I will go back repeatedly, because I know I'm going to get good food, and I like having a pleasant dining experience. With repeated visits, I achieve a rapport with the business and the people there, so I'll just keep returning unless or until I get tired of it.

Chez Panisse in Berkeley has been the place I've visited the most frequently. I just go and go and go and go, and then one day I wake up and I think, "Well, I've got that out of my system for a while." Then, sometime later, I'll just start in again. That restaurant has been such an important force in the food business. Many of us owe a debt to Alice Waters.

If someone who really cared about food came to Northern California to eat for a few days, I'd send them to Chez Panisse. Then I'd urge them to head north for Mendocino, stopping on the way at the New Boonville Hotel in Boonville, about thirty miles south of Mendocino. I have had some fine meals there, including my all-time favorite hamburger. They grind their own meat, bake the buns and grow the spinach they put on it. For an example of their innovative approach to cooking, see the Warm Salad recipe on page 134.

One of the two questions interviewers ask the most (the other relates to how we get all the elements of a meal to come together at the same time) deals with my last meal on earth. Permit me to indulge . . . .

My Last Meal

I would start backwards. The one thing I know for certain I'd want is the dessert, and I would want my mother to cook it. I love her cooking. The meal wouldn't be all that exotic. But it would end with a Grand Marnier soufflé that my mother made when I was nineteen, I still remember it.

I would want homemade bread. Maybe wheat, but probably white. I mean, who cares about health for the last meal?

For an appetizer, I remember when Kathi Riley made gravlox at the restaurant: fresh salmon cured with salt and sugar, which we served on toasted homemade rye bread spread with Mendocino Mustard. I'd have that.

Next, things become less exotic. I'd have roast chicken with little baked potatoes cooked in the same pan, carrots, and, since I'm not worrying about calories any more, stuffing, and some kind of scalloped potatoes. My propensity for carbohydrates is showing.

Then I'd have really young green beans. A simple salad of just-picked greens, with perfect olive oil. A dry white wine—perhaps Premier Reserve Chardonnay from Navarro Vineyards. Some Philipponnat champagne, and a good strong espresso (I won't have to worry about staying awake late) with a large bowl of Barbara Holzrichter's Grand Finale caramels—the ones with the nuts in them.

None of these things is fancy, but they would all be so perfect. That's all you ever need. You don't have to have truffles to be elegant or great or perfect. Some years ago, I would have included a good deal of chocolate. I'm not quite as much in love with it as I used to be. That's because I've already lived out my wildest chocolate fantasies in the restaurant.

My Next Meal

That's a much more pleasant concept than my final meal. I eat quite simply, and I think you'll find that to be the case with many cooks. The ones I know eat cold cereal for breakfast. Personally I prefer Grape Nuts. Yes, I know it's indistinguishable from cat food, but there's something about how crunchy it remains, even drenched in milk.

I don't patronize fast food franchises. I've tried them, as a cultural phenomenon, but while what they are doing is undeniably fast, I would not call it food. When a reporter asked me what I had had for lunch one day, the true answer was "tuna surprise." Stephanie Kroninger makes it for her daughter Eula, who has a tuna fetish that cannot be believed. Somehow that never got into the story. Too ordinary, I guess. But that's real life. Of course if I were to call it Surprise de Thon, then it would be all right for the reporters. Anyway, I've had it so many times, it isn't a surprise any more.

My Life Till Now

I come from a very academically-oriented background, and yet, given the sorts of things I was interested in, and the kinds of things I did as a child, it isn't all that surprising that I ended up running a restaurant.

A lot of people I know had horrible childhoods with regard to their culinary adventures. They were fed overcooked vegetables and lots of Wonder Bread with Skippy Peanut Butter and Welch's jelly. But that wasn't my experience. Food has always had an emphasis within my family, especially toward quality and good taste and attractive presentation.

For my first birthday, I am told, although I cannot remember it, my mother made me a Dobosh Torte, which is an extremely complicated multi-layer Hungarian cake. It is very rich, and is seen infrequently, because it is so labor intensive. In fact it has not been seen since in our

"We were living in Los Angeles when Margaret was small. I think we fed her well. We went for walks most evenings, and Margaret always wanted to go by the Baskin-Robbins. She usually ordered pistachio."

—Harold Fox
Margaret's Father

family, because my mother rarely tries the same experiment twice. My father still talks about it with a far-away look in his eyes.

I wonder if there is something related to imprinting here. Perhaps all children who are exposed to Hungarian pastry within seventy-two hours of their first birthday grow up to own restaurants.

In any event, with a beginning like that—and who knows what other food experiences I had in my first two years—how could I help but have an appreciation of good food?

I don't remember every meal I've ever eaten, but I can clearly remember the experience of having certain dishes. When I was four, my Hungarian grandmother always gave me coffee with milk and a lot of sugar, much to my mother's horror. I can vividly recall the experience of sitting at that kitchen table drinking what to me was nectar. It must have been bad *so* bad for me. I'd probably be twelve feet tall if I hadn't drunk that.

I remember going to visit my other grandmother when I was very little, and she made oatmeal for me. She taught all of us how to make and eat the oatmeal. How good it tasted. I have so many memories of the pleasure that food provides, and has always provided. I like to think that I am helping now to create memories for other people.

My father is a manufacturer's rep, and owns his own company. My mom was a Spanish major, but ended up teaching English as a second language. She writes and does copy editing. They're both bright, caring, and well-read people. There was no question in anybody's mind that my sister and I would go to college. I had assumed, ever since I'd turned fourteen, that I would be going on for a Ph.D. in clinical psychology.

Somehow in the midst of knowing precisely what I wanted to do, I also spent a lot of time cooking. My mom has collected a huge number of cookbooks. She's always been a good cook, and she still is. She has a research-oriented attitude toward food: what makes something good or bad, or work or not work.

So I wasn't the sort of person who made Bisquick biscuits from the recipe on the box. I always sought out new recipes. When I was seventeen and eighteen, I gave bread baking classes at the Unitarian Church in Kensington for about eighteen months, which was a wonderful experience.

My sister and I would cook things as presents for our parents. Special little anniversary dinners with chicken breasts and wild rice and some sort of exotic cherry bombe. Very sophisticated sorts of menus.

We also participated in a series of Christmas fairs at the Church. We made food the likes of which no one had ever seen. Fantastic and highly ornate animals. Shortbread lions with manes made from dough pushed through a garlic press. We spent weeks in preparation.

When I was nineteen and twenty, I lived with another family for a couple of years, and did a lot of cooking for them, and helped cater friends' functions. Then and now, I would rather do a party for sixty than a party for six.

At the University of California in Santa Cruz, I shared a house with six other people, There was always a lot of cooking to be done, and I found myself enjoying the task more and more.

In my senior year, after signing up to take the Graduate Record Exam three times and forfeiting my entry fee each time, I finally realized that I needed a break of some sort; that I wasn't ready to go right on into graduate school. So, soon after I got my B.A. in developmental psychology, I decided to go to Mendocino for a few months to get my head, or my act together. I'd never been there before, but the rest of the family had.

I wanted to get away from the city and the smog, and I especially wanted to get away from Santa Cruz, because I saw so many people who just stayed in their college town forever, and grew into it more and more and never changed. I didn't want that easy way out.

I arrived in Mendocino around Labor Day, 1975, just as the tourists were leaving (they left earlier then), and within three hours of arriving, I had a job as a baker at the Men-

"I try not to get drawn into notions about mysterious happenings, but I still have the post card that I sent to Margaret when Harold and I went to Mendocino for a brief vacation in 1972. I wrote, 'This is a beautiful place, and I hope it will become part of your life someday.' "
—Anne Fox

"You know, you
sometimes just
accept things when
they come along,
and then looking
back on it later you
think, that kid did
some amazing
things. In fact,
Margaret was only
ten or eleven when
I had her taking
orders for my
business over the
telephone. I paid
her twenty cents for
every one she got
right. I like to think
that some of her
business acumen
may have been
fostered in that
way."

—Harold Fox

docino Hotel and a little apartment at the Art Center. It turned out that I was happy as a clam there, and it was soon apparent to me that I had no intention of leaving.

Bill Zacha, founder of the Art Center, mentioned that it would be nice to have something good to eat at the evening film programs, and so Congo Bars (see page 206) were born: my first independent commercial venture.

There was little room for growth at the Hotel, and I was paid a small amount of money for doing a good job. I moved over to The Cheese Shop, where I was given *carte blanche* to do what I wanted in the way of extra-curricular baking. They were happy to sell my truffles, croissants, little fussy cookies, fruitcake, and panforte. Between that baking and my Congo Bars, I had the opportunity to see what it was like to have my stuff out there in the world, and it felt good.

Then along came the opportunity to buy Cafe Beaujolais and the rest, as they say, is history.

We had our personal and our financial problems, as recounted previously, and my parents wrung their hands a lot—but they were also wonderfully supportive, with money and energy and advice and love.

My Life Now

The restaurant is, of course, the dominant factor in my life now. There is hardly a day when I have to think, "What am I going to do today because the Beaujolais is closed." It may not sound exciting, yet I find it a full and enriching and rewarding life. It is extremely varied in nature and scope, and I keep learning and learning. I've become a lot more sophisticated as a businesswoman. I know what has to be done for the business to run smoothly and happily, and causing this to happen is my main restaurant-related goal these days.

One of the really enjoyable things about running my own show is having the chance to express myself. I like to think that the style and operation of the restaurant is an extension of my personality; the sort of place that tends, I hope, to be insouciant—an upbeat and happy place. I don't find it at all boring, or a grind, and I don't think the staff does either.

Now there are two new elements for me to deal with: expansion into mail order and wholesale activities, and my becoming a more public personality.

On Being a Public Person

Most of the time I like it, because basically I'm a ham and I do like people. But then, at a certain point, I *stop* liking it, because I am also a private person—and I get shy. What I'm coming to realize is that when you become a public person, you don't really have a lot of choice, unless you physically remove yourself from the sort of situation where you're going to be in the public eye. But *I'm* the one who has to start setting the limits. The minute I put myself out on the road saying, "Hi there, I'm a public person," everyone takes me at my word.

I really *do* like people a lot. I'm not out there in public a great deal waving my hands and blowing kisses from the car, or even from the back of the dining room. There are some owners or cooks or both who make several grand entrances in the course of the day to receive the plaudits of the dining masses. I may walk around to see how everything is going, but no one sprinkles rose petals in my path.

One of the major pitfalls in this world, I am convinced, is believing too much of your own publicity. You have to watch out for a certain kind of hubris, and not fly too close to the sun. This topic came up with regard to the ways and means of publicizing this book. I could not live with a press release that talked about "one of America's great chefs now reveals all . . . ." And yet a book by "this nice lady who runs a pleasant little restaurant in some rural village," would not sell many books. Somewhere in between lies the place where the truth and the best things to say overlap. That's what we have to go for.

Social Life

When I'm not at the restaurant, I'm kind of at a loss as to what to do. On days when I'm not cooking breakfast, I'll

still get into town by 6:30 a.m., but then I'll walk around the village for half an hour or forty-five minutes. This is a good thing to do. It forces me to be outside, and to take advantage of the beautiful area I'm always being reminded I live in, but rarely see. I don't really get out too often during the day. I tend to get focused, fixated you might say, and I must finish what I've started, which can easily take the whole day and then some.

Still, I am convinced that meeting people in social circumstances is both necessary to my own well-being, and probably beneficial to the restaurant as well, since so much of my social life revolves around restaurant people. Many of the friends I've made in recent years are in the food business in one capacity or another.

Most of this socializing goes on in San Francisco and its vicinity. When I have or can make a little free time, I'll often head for the big city, where I seem to spend a lot of time in other people's restaurants. A well-run restaurant is an enjoyable place for me to be. To eat, and to talk.

What do we talk about? We all know so much about each others' businesses, we don't have go through the common questions we get from others, such as, "How did you get into the business?" and "How do you know how much to order?" We talk about staff problems and interesting suppliers we've found and recipes and plans for expansion. Shop talk for the most part.

Where Things Are Going

I don't have a five-year or a twenty-year life plan. I made my age twenty-five goal, and I have no more age-related goals. Now that the restaurant has a really strong core of staff whom I trust, and a manager who's extremely competent, I've branched off into a second business called Cafe Beaujolais Bakery. The Bakery is an entirely separate entity which produces an Italian-style candy called Panforte di Mendocino and a fruitcake, with more products to come.

I'm doing this and I'm loving it, because even though it was never a grand and conscious plan, it turns out that involvement in the bakery is a perfect counterpart to my restaurant life. While it still focuses on the food business, which I love, it is different in almost every way. It has few employees while the restaurant has many. We know exactly what products we're going to make months in advance, instead of deciding every morning. It is very seasonal, so we can plan well ahead. We know that October through December will be our busiest times. In the restaurant, we interact with a lot of people every day, which is rewarding but is also quite a strain at times. In the Bakery, we have limited contacts with the outside world, selling by mail order and at the wholesale level only.

So the restaurant and the bakery will keep me going for a while. Perhaps a long while. In about forty years, I'll be as old as Colonel Sanders was when he *started* his business. I've got time.

But in this life, it seems that good ideas keep arising. They dance around in my mind enchanting and beguiling. And once they have made themselves known to me there's no other choice but to consider them seriously. I don't think I could *ever* devise a plan that would let me anticipate realistically what I will be doing in five years. That seems inconceivable. For life to be meaningful, exciting, and fun, it is desirable—indeed I would say essential—to keep myself open to all events and all possibilities at all times.

RECIPES

 # Soups

CHICKEN STOCK

Makes 8 cups or 2 quarts

I enjoy the process of making chicken stock. At the restaurant, we make many, many gallons every week. We keep two 40-quart stock pots going constantly. Canned chicken stock always tastes phony to me. It is salted and often has MSG in it. It's rather presumptuous of the manufacturers to put that in. I don't add salt unless it's an ingredient in the preparation of the final dish.

One should really get in the habit of saving leftover chicken parts—backs, gizzards, necks, all that. The carcasses of chickens, cooked or raw. Save them in the freezer, and when you have enough, make stock. This stock freezes well.

10 cups water	several parsley sprigs
4 lbs. chicken parts	2 bay leaves
2 onions, cut into quarters	freshly ground pepper
2 stalks celery, cut into chunks	⅛ lemon
2 carrots, cut into slices	

Place all ingredients in 6-quart pot. Bring to a boil. Skim the grey foam off and reduce heat. After 15 minutes, skim foam off again. Simmer for 2½ hours, partially covered.

Strain, remove as much fat as possible with a large spoon, and chill overnight. Remove the rest of the fat fastidiously.

This stock will keep indefinitely if you boil it for 10 minutes every 3 days—but since that will reduce the quantity each time, it probably makes sense to freeze any stock you won't be using promptly.

WATERCRESS AND POTATO SOUP

The reason I make this stems from stems. I had made a watercress salad for dinner, and found that I had a lot of stems and nonperfect leaves left over. It seemed such a waste to throw this stuff out. I hypothesized that since watercress is naturally peppery, there was enough flavor in the stems to make a soup. I put the whole thing together in about 20 minutes. Of course you could make this with perfectly fine watercress (but if you've got perfectly fine watercress, it's really much better to make a salad of it, and then make this soup from the leftover parts).

1¾ cups chopped onions

¼ cup unsalted butter

2 cups potatoes (any kind), chopped, peeled, and diced

5 cups Chicken Stock (see page 117)

½ tsp white pepper

1 tsp salt

4 cups firmly packed watercress stems + not-so-perfect leaves

Crème Fraîche (see page 244), sour cream, or lightly whipped cream

Sauté onions in butter for 10 minutes, or until onions are translucent. Add potatoes, chicken stock, pepper, and salt. Bring to a boil, then reduce heat and simmer for 10 minutes, or until potatoes are soft. Add watercress and simmer for an additional 5 to 8 minutes.

Place soup in a blender and blend until homogenized. Pour through a strainer into another container.

Serve with crème fraîche (whipped or liquid), sour cream, or lightly whipped cream.

SPRING PEA SOUP

Makes 10 cups.
Serves 7

It's a little hypocritical to call this "Spring" because we use frozen peas—*petits pois*, the expensive little frozen ones. In fact, at the restaurant, we call it "Name That Season Pea Soup." It just tastes *so* good—better than anything you could imagine frozen peas tasting like. You just dump all the ingredients together, blend it, and in about 20 minutes, you have wonderful, fresh-smelling, intensely green soup.

½ cup butter
1 large yellow onion, chopped
2 Tb flour
1 tsp curry powder
¼ tsp white pepper
5 cups Chicken Stock, heated (see page 117)
3¾ cups peas (frozen *petits pois* work well)

1½ tsp sugar
1½ cups half and half
1½ tsp salt
½ cup frozen chopped spinach
½ cup heavy cream or Crème Fraîche (see page 244)
½ tsp lemon rind, grated

Sauté onion in butter over medium heat for 5 minutes, or until onion is translucent. Add flour and cook for 3 minutes stirring constantly. Add pepper, salt, and chicken stock. Bring to a boil while stirring, scraping bottom.

Simmer for 5 minutes, add peas, sugar, and spinach, and simmer 8 to 10 minutes. Purée, strain, and add half and half. Warm gently. This must not boil.

Whip cream or crème fraîche and lemon rind until soft peaks form. Serve soup in heated bowls with a dollop of whipped cream or crème fraîche.

SPINACH SOUP HYSTERIQUE

In certain respects, running a restaurant is a process you have to make easier than it sounds, or the entire staff would collapse. So we try to become really efficient at what we do. And I think efficiency, combined with turning out a product that's very good, is something that can be passed on to the person at home. You know, it doesn't have to take 5 days of preparation in order for something to be good. One of the best soups I ever made was done in 20 minutes, when we ran out of soup for dinner and I whipped up this spinach soup amid much hysteria—all the blenders going full blast—and it came out great.

It has to do with my belief that you should try to dispel mystique, rather than try to build it up. . .and in the very act of dispelling, I guess you create a whole new *kind* of mystique, which is the "there *is* no mystique" mystique.

So this soup fits that philosophy. It is, needless to say, incredibly fast and simple to make, and awfully good.

1 large onion, chopped
¼ cup unsalted butter
5 cups Chicken Stock (see page 117)
2 Tb uncooked white rice
1 11-oz. box frozen spinach, thawed and drained

1½ tsp salt
½ tsp white pepper
¼ tsp ground nutmeg
sour cream or Crème Fraîche (see page 244) for topping

Sauté onion in butter until it is translucent, about 5 minutes. Add chicken stock, bring to a boil, add rice, turn down, and simmer for 20 minutes. Add spinach and seasonings, and continue simmering for 5 minutes. Blend in blender, then pour through a strainer. Serve with sour cream or crème fraîche.

ZUCCHINI-CURRY SOUP

Makes 8 cups.
Serves 5 to 6.

This is a real standby soup which takes almost no time whatsoever to prepare. You don't have to spend time sautéing or mixing onions. You just mix it together and it comes out delightfully.

The curry powder is an essential ingredient, and I really don't recommend using the cheap stuff from the supermarket. It often has an unpleasant harsh flavor. Various friends of the restaurant prepare magnificent versions.

Chive blossoms are those little flowers—purple balls actually—that are, not surprisingly, the blossoms of the chive plant. You can eat them. They taste like chives! When we serve them in the restaurant and tell people they can eat the flowers, they usually say, "Oh, don't be silly." Then they eat the flowers and love them.

4 zucchini, cut into thick slices
1 onion, chopped
1 Tb curry powder (excellent quality)
3 cups Chicken Stock (see page 117)
salt

pepper
¾ cup half and half
½ cup whipped Crème Fraîche (see page 244)
½ cup chopped chives
chive blossoms (if available)

Place zucchini, onion, curry powder, and chicken stock in a saucepan. Cover and simmer for 25 minutes. Stir occasionally. Purée mixture in a blender, strain, add salt and pepper to taste, and half and half.

Serve in heated bowls with a dollop of whipped crème fraîche, a sprinkling of chopped chives, and, if possible, a chive blossom per bowl.

TOMATO BISQUE

Makes 9 cups

This is the epitome of a comforting soup. I would serve it three times a week if I could get away with it, especially during our long winters, with their grey, overcast days. It's creamy and rich and nourishing. Even though I am such a fan of fresh tomatoes, this is the one dish that I think may even work better with canned tomatoes.

½ cup chopped onions
½ cup unsalted butter
1 tsp dill seed
1½ tsp dill weed
1½ tsp Beaujolais Blend Herbs (see page 256) or oregano
5 cups tomatoes (preferably canned crushed whole tomatoes)
4 cups Chicken Stock (see page 117)

2 Tb flour
2 tsp salt
½ tsp white pepper
¼ cup chopped parsley
4 tsp honey
1¼ cups heavy cream
⅔ cup half and half
sour cream

In a large pot, sauté onions in 6 tablespoons butter along with dill seed, dill weed, and herbs for 5 minutes, or until onions are translucent. Add tomatoes and chicken stock and heat.

Make a roux by blending 2 tablespoons butter and 2 tablespoons flour, whisking constantly over medium heat for 3 minutes, without browning. Add roux to stock and whisk to blend. Add salt and pepper. Bring to a boil, stirring occasionally. Reduce heat and simmer for 15 minutes. Add chopped parsley, honey, cream and half and half. Remove from heat and purée. Strain. When ready to serve, reheat and serve with a dollop of sour cream.

GARLIC SOUP

Makes about 7 cups.
Serves 5 generously

The garlic flavor doesn't come across sharply because the garlic is cooked so long. The soup has a mellow flavor that one doesn't normally associate with garlic. The ingredients are inexpensive, except for the saffron, which is optional, and you just need a teeny bit, anyway. Basically you could put this recipe together with just garlic, olive oil, egg yolks, and water.

A few words about sun-dried tomatoes: The ones you find in gourmet food stores usually come from Italy. They're dried in the sun until they are prune-like, then put in olive oil. They have a very intense flavor that I don't associate with the average tomato. You can make them yourself (see page 167). I want to put them in everything.

Eight words about goat cheese: Laura Chenel's California Chèvre. It's my favorite kind.

When prepared with water, the broth can be used as a base for vegetarian soups. The dish is delicious, satisfying, cheap, and healthy—and keeps were-wolves away from the door.

2 quarts Chicken Stock (see page 117) or water
2 bulbs of garlic, separated into cloves, not peeled
2 tsp salt
1/4 tsp freshly ground pepper
1/4 tsp thyme
2 cloves
2 bay leaves
6 sprigs parsley
2 Tb olive oil

2 pinches saffron
15 croûtes (A croûte is a slice of baguette 1/4 inch thick, dried in 300 degree oven for 20 to 25 minutes)
4 oz. grated Asiago or Parmesan cheese or 4 oz. goat cheese
3 Tb puréed sun-dried tomatoes (see page 167)
1 egg yolk
2 Tb olive oil

Boil the chicken stock or water, garlic, salt, pepper, thyme, cloves, bay leaves, parsley, olive oil, and optional saffron together slowly for 45 minutes. Then strain, pushing garlic through a sieve back into the broth.

Spread each croûte evenly with some tomato purée, and top generously with grated Asiago or Parmesan. If you use goat cheese, first spread it onto croûte and then sprinkle tomatoes on top. Press into cheese. Place croûtes on large flat pan and bake at 325 degrees for 5 to 8 minutes.

While baking, whisk the egg yolks for one minute while slowly adding the olive oil, as you would for mayonnaise.

When ready to serve, place a generous spoonful of the mayonnaise in the bottom of a heated soup bowl. Add hot soup and stir briefly. Top with 3 warmed cheese croûtes.

CREAMY MUSHROOM SOUP

This recipe is interesting, because you can make it just as well with either chicken stock, or with a vegetarian broth. It's really hearty either way, and has a good strong mushroom taste. I prefer a brand of vegetable broth cubes called Hugli, which can be found in health food stores. (We get it at Corners of the Mouth in Mendocino.) It has a very distinctive flavor and is not at all watery. If you can't find Hugli, you can use another brand. Fresh mushrooms only, please.

1¾ lbs. sliced raw mushrooms
½ cup unsalted butter
⅓ cup chopped green onions
5 cloves garlic, peeled
3 Tb flour
6 cups Chicken Stock (see page 117) or 6 cups Hugli broth (4 Hugli cubes with 6 cups hot water)

¾ cup heavy cream
1 tsp fresh or ½ tsp dried tarragon or dill
¼ cup Crème Fraîche (see page 244)
1 egg yolk
1 Tb lemon juice
1 tsp salt
1 Tb Marsala, optional

Step 1: Sauté vegetables

Sauté mushrooms in ¼ cup butter for 5 minutes. Add green onions and garlic, and continue sautéing for 1 more minute. Set aside.

Step 2: Make roux

Make a roux from the remaining ¼ cup butter and the flour. (A roux is a cooked flour and butter paste that's the base for sauces.) Cook the roux for 4 minutes over medium heat, whisking constantly. Don't let the roux brown.

Step 3: Make soup

Add either the chicken stock or Hugli broth to the roux, bring to a boil stirring frequently with a whisk, then simmer for 5 minutes. Add mushrooms and simmer for 15 minutes more. Purée the mushroom mixture and add the heavy cream. Add the tarragon or dill, salt, and optional Marsala.

Step 4: Make liaison and serve

Stir together the crème fraîche, egg yolk, and lemon juice to make the liaison.

Pour soup into heated bowls. Dribble the liaison into the soup to form the design of your choice. (We usually make ours look a bit esoteric—sort of New Wave.)

CLAM CHOWDER

Makes 8 cups.
Serves 6

I was never too crazy about clams, but this recipe has turned me into a clam fan. This chowder is a typical New England or Boston style white clam chowder, and it's satisfying and delicious. Don't stint on the ingredients. It's important to use all half and half. Sally Kotch and Sam Shook, two expert and influential chowder makers, insist upon that.

4 slices bacon, coarsely chopped
3 green onions, chopped
5 medium red potatoes, unpeeled, cut into ½-inch cubes
⅓ cup chopped green pepper
⅓ cup sliced celery
3 cloves minced garlic
1 cup cold water

1 cup clam juice (bottled is OK)
1 tsp salt
½ tsp white pepper
1 tsp Worcestershire sauce
2 drops Tabasco sauce
3 6½-oz. cans clams, with juice
2 cups half and half

Coarsely chop bacon and sauté until crisp. Drain off half the fat and discard. Add onions, potatoes, green pepper, celery and garlic to chopped bacon and remaining bacon fat. Add water and clam juice, salt, pepper, Worcestershire and Tabasco sauces. Cover and simmer for 15 minutes, or until potatoes are tender.

In a separate pan, heat the clams in their juice and add to other mixture, along with the half and half. *Do not boil!*

Serve in heated bowls.

FRESH SALMON CHOWDER

In Mendocino, we have an abundance of such luxury items as salmon and raspberries. In other places, everybody thinks they're really special—but we actually reach a point where we grow tired of them.

I love this recipe because it can take so many different forms. It can be made with rice, it can be made with potatoes. It can be made with garlic, if you feel like it. It can have saffron (I *do* love saffron). It can have sour cream. It takes a little longer to prepare than most soups, but the ingredients are all so simple—that is, if you can get all the salmon you want.

You'll need to make salmon stock, which is really no problem, especially for people who don't like to throw anything away. Even if you're a fabulous skinner, there will still be plenty of meat left on the bones, plus the head, and the tail to flavor the stock. So it all goes into the pot with some vegetables, and in less than an hour, you come out with great stock.

STOCK

carcass from 1 salmon (including head and tail)

14 cups water

2 stalks celery, coarsely chopped

2 peeled carrots, coarsely chopped

2 onions, coarsely chopped

1 bay leaf

CHOWDER

salmon filet(s) to equal 1 lb., skin scaled

1 onion, finely chopped

¼ cup unsalted butter

3 pinches saffron (optional)

3 cloves garlic, minced

½ tsp Beaujolais Blend Herbs (or ¼ tsp dried oregano and ¼ tsp dried basil, or ½ tsp fresh oregano and ½ tsp fresh basil)

¾ cup thinly sliced celery

1 cup thinly sliced carrots

¾ cup peeled and diced (½-inch cubes) potatoes, uncooked *or* ⅔ cup uncooked long grain white rice

1 cup dry white wine

2 Tb minced parsley

salmon stock from above recipe

8 thin lemon slices, seeded

sour cream

Step 1: Make salmon stock

Place stock ingredients in a pot, bring to a boil, and simmer for 40 minutes, occasionally skimming the grey foam from the surface. Strain and discard bones and vegetables.

Step 2: Poach salmon

Bring salmon stock to a near simmer, and immerse filet(s), poaching 5 minutes for each inch of thickness of the piece. (A 1-inch piece would cook 5 minutes; a 2-inch piece 10 minutes, etc. This is half the cooking time needed for fully cooked salmon, but it will finish cooking from the heat of the chowder). Warning: Overcooked salmon is a little like salmon-flavored sawdust. When done, remove from stock with a slotted spoon or metal spatula, remove skin, and cool. Separate fish into small chunks, not small flaky pieces like tuna.

Step 3: Cook vegetables

In a 4 quart saucepan, sauté onions and herbs in butter until onions are translucent (about 5 minutes). Add garlic and optional saffron, celery, carrots, and rice or potatoes. Pour in white wine and salmon stock. Simmer for 15 or 20 minutes (test rice or potatoes for done-ness).

Add salmon chunks and simmer gently for 3 to 5 minutes. Serve immediately in heated bowls with a slice of lemon per bowl, a dollop of sour cream, and parsley sprinkled on top.

CHILLED BULGARIAN CUCUMBER SOUP

Makes 9 cups.
Serves 6

This recipe was made by Kathi Riley, a friend of mine from San Francisco, who cooked at the Beaujolais one summer. It's a very simple and immensely refreshing soup. It's perfect when you're sitting out on the deck, especially on those rare hot days we get on the coast. Kathi has come in to cook at times when I've had to leave, and when I come back, I'm always delighted by what she's made, because she's got an imaginative style, and everything she makes tastes really good. This soup is an excellent example. I'm not at all sure what's Bulgarian about this.

5 large cucumbers, peeled, seeded, and minced

2 large cloves garlic, peeled and minced

½ cup green onions, minced

juice of 1 lemon

1 quart buttermilk

½ cup sour cream

1 cup plain yogurt

1½ Tb chopped fresh dill or ¾ tsp dried dill

1 tsp salt

¼ tsp white pepper

½ cup chopped, toasted walnuts

With a wooden spoon, mix together all ingredients except walnuts and let sit, covered, in the refrigerator for at least 4 hours, or as long as 24 hours. To serve, stir, ladle into chilled soup bowls, and sprinkle with walnuts.

MUSHROOM, SPINACH AND RICE RAMEN NOODLE SOUP

Serves 4 generously

Michael Gabel, a vegetarian who devised this soup, owns an energy-consulting firm in Berkeley. He created this tasty recipe to fit into his busy schedule. The ingredients called for can be purchased at most health food stores or Oriental food markets.

10 cups water
1 piece fresh ginger (the size of a walnut), coarsely chopped
¼ tsp white pepper
2 Tb tamari soy sauce
1 bunch green onions, chopped
1 onion, chopped
1 small carrot, thinly sliced
4 cloves garlic, minced
2 Tb sesame oil

4 Tb light miso (not too salty)
3 oz. dried brown rice ramen noodles
½ lb. mushrooms, sliced
1 yellow crookneck squash, sliced
¼ lb. green beans, French cut
10 oz. tofu
2 cups cauliflower, thinly sliced
¾ lb. fresh spinach, chopped

Simmer together water, ginger, pepper, and soy sauce for 15 minutes. Strain; discard ginger but retain liquid ginger-water.

Sauté green onions, onion, carrot, and garlic in sesame oil for 5 to 7 minutes. Add ginger water and miso. Bring to a boil. Put in ramen noodles, mushrooms, squash, beans, tofu, and cauliflower. Bring to a boil, and boil gently for 5 minutes.

Add spinach and simmer for 1 to 2 minutes. Serve immediately in heated bowls.

PEPPERY SHRIMP DUMPLING SOUP WITH CHINESE GREENS ©

Serves 8 to 10 as a first course, 4 to 5 as a main course

These next two recipes, and their introductions, come from my friend Barbara Tropp, author of *The Modern Art of Chinese Cooking* (Morrow) and chef/owner of China Moon, a Chinese bistro in San Francisco.

"For certain, one of the reasons I opened my own restaurant was so that I'd have an iron-clad excuse not to cater Chinese dinners at my friend Margaret's Cafe Beaujolais! I loved what had become an annual Mendocino event, but the sudden appearance of woks, cleavers, steamers and mysterious Chinese vegetables and condiments set everyone into a tizzy. Nonetheless, great dishes came out of those occasions, and here is one of them: a nice peppery soup chock-full of fat dumplings stuffed with shrimp and fresh waterchestnuts. I prefer greens with a bit of sharp tang to offset the sweetness of the dumpling filling. If nothing Chinese is available, use tender watercress or even spinach. If fresh waterchestnuts are not to be had, substitute jicama or green apples. Serves 4 to 5 as a one-bowl meal with a crisp salad and toasty baguette, and 8 to 10 as a prelude to a multicourse meal."

¾ lb. fresh shrimp in shells, peeled and deveined

1½ Tb finely minced fresh ginger

3 to 4 Tb finely minced green and white scallions

2 tsp old-fashioned kosher salt

⅛ tsp freshly ground pepper

1 Tb Chinese rice wine or dry sherry

1½ tsp lard or chicken fat in a tepid, liquid state

5 fresh waterchestnuts, cut into tiny, peppercorn-sized dices (to yield ¼ cup)

50 paper-thin won ton wrappers

3 to 4 cups fresh, trimmed greens (baby bok choy, spinach, watercress)

8 cups Chicken Stock (see page 117), seasoned to taste with Roasted Szechwan Pepper-Salt (recipe follows)

In a food processor fitted with a steel S-blade, blend the shrimp, ginger, scallion, salt, pepper, wine and fat to a smooth paste. Then stir in waterchestnuts by hand. (Alternatively, mince the shrimp to a near paste by hand and combine with the remaining ingredients.) Poach a dab of filling in sim-

© Recipe and notes copyright 1984 by Barbara Tropp

mering unsalted water until white, taste, and adjust seasoning if necessary with salt or pepper.

To form dumplings, brush the rim of a won-ton wrapper lightly with water. Put about ½ teaspoon filling in the center, then seal the wrapper shut in whatever fashion you like. I prefer to pinch-pleat it shut in a little 'bag.' Put the dumplings aside on a lightly floured baking sheet.

When all the dumplings are made, poach them in a generous amount of boiling unsalted water for 1½ minutes, then drain and spread in a single layer on a large platter. At this point, the dumplings can be left to cool then bagged airtight and refrigerated for up to 3 days. Bring to room temperature before using.

To make the soup, blanch the greens for 10 seconds in boiling, unsalted water, drain promptly, chill under cold water, and press gently to remove excess water.

Portion the greens among heated bowls. Bring the stock to a simmer, season it, then add the dumplings for a minute or so more to heat them through. Divide the dumplings and stock among the bowls and serve.

ROASTED SZECHWAN PEPPER-SALT ©   *Makes ¼ cup*

"Of the several things I leave behind in the wake of a Chinese dinner I have prepared at Cafe Beaujolais—a forgotten steamer lid, dry cellophane noodles sprinkled liberally around the restaurant, an extra tin of soy sauce—I invariably 'present' the kitchen with a jar of pepper-salt. It is an all-purpose seasoning, excellent with fresh-steamed corn, burgers and even popcorn, as well as Chinese food.

Szechwan peppercorns are hollow brown peppercorns with a numbing quality and irresistible aroma. Old-fashioned kosher salt is very mild; if you cannot find it, use half the amount of fine sea salt."

2 Tb Szechwan brown peppercorns   **¼ cup old-fashioned kosher salt**

Combine the peppercorns and salt in a dry, heavy skillet. Set over moderately low heat and stir until the peppercorns are fragrant and the salt turns off-white, 3 to 4 minutes. The peppercorns will smoke; do not let them scorch. Crush the hot mixture to a powder in a mortar, then sieve to remove peppercorn husks. Store airtight in glass jar, away from light, heat, and humidity.

HOT AND SPICY SOUP

Serves 6 to 8

Debbie Slutsky is a cook, a food consultant, and one of the most organized people I've ever met. She can whip a kitchen into shape in no time flat. She also manages to be very human and maintain a sense of humor—difficult qualities, especially in a professional kitchen.

This is Debbie's version of a classic Northern Chinese soup.

½ cup olive oil

¼ cup finely minced garlic

2½ tsp finely minced serrano or other hot peppers

1 Tb finely minced ginger

2 cups day-old French bread, trimmed of all crusts and crumbled finely

1½ tsp cayenne pepper

6 cups Chicken Stock (see page 117)

⅓ cup lime juice

2 eggs, beaten

2 Tb chopped cilantro

salt   pepper

Heat olive oil in a heavy 3- to 4-quart saucepan. Add garlic, peppers, and ginger, and cook until soft but not browned. Add bread and stir well to coat with garlic mixture. Add cayenne and stock, and bring to a boil.

Turn heat down to moderate, and let simmer for ½ hour uncovered. Add lime juice and taste for seasonings, adding salt and pepper as needed.

When ready to serve, very slowly stir in beaten eggs, being sure not to let soup boil, otherwise the eggs will curdle. Stir in cilantro, pour into heated bowls, and serve immediately.

 # Salads

WALNUT VINAIGRETTE AND SALAD

Serves 4

Formerly-exotic oils are becoming more available these days, which is good news for cooks. I find walnut oil makes a dressing that is a fresh, light complement to richer dishes such as the gnocchi (page 146). This dressing can also be made with hazelnut oil and hazelnuts instead of walnut oil and walnuts.

1 cup toasted walnut halves
½ cup walnut oil
2 Tb lemon juice, strained
½ tsp salt
a few grinds of black pepper

¼ tsp Dijon mustard (optional)
butter lettuce for 4, or a mixture of lettuce, watercress and chopped Belgian endive; washed, dried, crisp, and cold.

Toast walnuts for 10 minutes in a 350 degeree oven. Rub skins off by tossing in a strainer. Combine oil, lemon juice, salt and pepper, and optional mustard. Place greens and walnuts in bowl. Toss with dressing.

Serve on chilled plates.

WARM SALAD

Forty miles southeast of Mendocino is the even-smaller town of Boonville, and it is there that Charlene and Vernon Rollins have established an almost magical restaurant. It's a complete little eco-system. They raise their own animals and grow their own vegetables. This distinctive recipe epitomizes the unique style of the New Boonville Hotel. Use a grill for best results.

2 rabbit loins

2 whole rabbit livers

2 quarts mixed bitter or strongly flavored greens (e.g., a variety of red and green chicories, curly endive, Chinese mustard greens no more than 3 inches long, rocket leaves, pepper grass, watercress, and very crisp spinach leaves, washed and dried thoroughly)

juice of 2 lemons, strained

1 Tb Balsamic vinegar

1 cup small, freshly picked brussels sprouts (no more than ½ inch in diameter)

1 cup water

2 Tb unsalted butter

8 slices smoked bacon, cut in ½-inch pieces

⅔ cup olive or walnut oil

1 tsp finely-chopped garlic

salt and pepper

Grill rabbit loins, leaving all the fat around the kidney to baste the meat as it cooks. When cooked, bone them, cut away the fat, and cut meat into thin slices. Chop up the fat and reserve it.

Put the livers on the grill until rare. When cooked, cut into julienned strips. Put strips plus any juices released during cutting into a bowl, along with the sliced loin meat.

Place greens in a big bowl. Season with salt and pepper. Sprinkle with lemon juice and vinegar.

Place brussels sprouts in a pan with water, unsalted butter, salt and pepper. Cook until just tender, and drain. Place in bowl with the livers and loin meat.

Sauté bacon in oil, along with reserved rabbit fat, until crisp. At the last moment, add garlic, swirling just until garlic is cooked.

Immediately pour the contents of the sauté pan (bacon, garlic, oil and rabbit fat) into salad bowl. Mix with two wooden spoons until the heat is dispersed enough to use your hands to mix thoroughly.

Heap salad onto large warm plates, leveling off the tops. Divide the brussels sprouts and rabbit mixture evenly among the plates, on top of the leveled off greens. Serve immediately.

SPINACH-APPLE SALAD

Serves 5 to 6

I met Tom Mathews as he was giving me a bear hug, exclaiming that the green chile omelette he'd just finished was the best of his life. "Have we been introduced?" I remember thinking. Tom and his wife Nancy are now my good friends. They escaped from the city to an apple farm near Sebastopol, and have become quite expert in doing interesting things with apples. This salad is one of Nancy's inventions. If Rome or Jonathan apples are not available, then any nice tart apple, such as Pippins, will do.

1 lb. fresh spinach, trimmed and washed	1 tsp dry mustard
3 small Rome or Jonathan apples, coarsely chopped	1 tsp sugar
¼ cup toasted sunflower seeds	½ tsp salt
⅔ cup corn oil	2 tsp fresh lemon juice
¼ cup wine vinegar	2 dashes Tabasco sauce
2 Tb light soy sauce	freshly ground pepper

In a pint jar, shake all ingredients except spinach, apples and sunflower seeds. Toss spinach and apples with enough dressing to coat well, and add sunflower seeds.

RED CABBAGE SALAD

Serves 6

This salad recipe comes from my friend Penelope Wisner, a former food editor of *House and Garden*, now with the Simi Winery. She is seriously involved in the world of food and wine, and that includes wine vinegar. In many ways, Penelope is typical of people in the food and wine business: extremely knowledgeable, creative, and great fun to be with. It's hard to be a grouch when you're involved in such pleasure-giving activities.

The Balsamic vinegar called for is an Italian vinegar, aged in oak casks. It has a deep delicious flavor, and is enjoying something of a heyday in the gourmet food world.

½ head red cabbage
salt
freshly ground black pepper
½ cup parsley, finely chopped
2 Tb sherry wine vinegar or Balsamic vinegar

¼ cup (or more) olive oil
1 cup toasted walnuts
2 oz. Roquefort or bleu cheese

Cut cabbage in half. Cut out the core and discard. Chop the cabbage into very thin pieces, and place in a bowl with the parsley. Season with salt and pepper. Heat the vinegar in a small pot, and when it is very hot, pour over the cabbage. Quickly toss, coating each piece thoroughly. The cabbage will brighten in color.

Add the olive oil, and toss again. Taste for a balance of oil, vinegar, and seasonings. Add walnuts, and crumble in the Roquefort or bleu cheese. Toss and serve.

COLD TOSSED NOODLES WITH MESQUITE-GRILLED CHICKEN

*Serves 6 as an
appetizer,
4 as an entrée*

Loxie Devin is a talented cook who devised this recipe when working in the kitchen at Cafe Beaujolais during the summer of 1983. The peach flavor complements the mesquite-flavored chicken in an unexpectedly wonderful way. There's a good blending of both flavors and textures: richness from the cashews, sweetness from the peaches, and the sort of smoky flavor from the chicken.

Cooled thin noodles are becoming increasingly popular, and deservedly so. Mesquite charcoal or mesquite wood is to be found in more and more markets and gourmet shops, but if you can't find any, nonmesquite grilling is better than none at all.

2 whole chicken breasts grilled over mesquite wood or charcoal until done (bones left in)

3 Tb Balsamic vinegar

1 tsp Dijon mustard

½ tsp salt

½ tsp pepper

¾ cup light olive oil

2 fresh ripe peaches, peeled and pitted or ⅓ cup peach jam

½ lb. angel hair pasta (capellini), cooked, rinsed, drained, and cooled

2⅓ cup toasted cashews

leaves from 1 bunch cilantro

Remove chicken from bones. Reserve meat. Cover bones with 2 cups water, and simmer for 1 hour. Remove bones from liquid. Carefully remove all chicken fat and continue to simmer until liquid is reduced to to ¼ cup.

To make dressing, place vinegar, mustard, salt, pepper, chicken stock reduction, peaches or peach jam, and olive oil in the bowl of a food processor. Blend until peaches are liquefied. Toss dressing, pasta, chicken, and cashews together until blended. Divide evenly among plates. Garnish with cilantro leaves and serve.

CHINESE CHICKEN SALAD

Serves 6 to 8

This is one of the most popular things we've ever served at Cafe Beaujolais. It's a blend of different flavors and different textures that is immensely satisfying. Sally Koch introduced this dish to our kitchen.

It's not hard to make, but it has a lot of steps. However you don't have to do it all at once. You can make the marinade and the dressing well in advance—but you should use the rice sticks on the day you fry them. (Rice sticks are dry noodles made from processed rice and water. They come in coils and look like really thin, transparent spaghetti. You'll find them in Oriental food stores, and even in the exotic foods department of many supermarkets. Get the Five Spice powder at the same places.) You break off a clump of rice sticks and throw it into very hot oil. In just a few seconds, it expands dramatically into crispy, fluffy, white noodles. But because there is so little to them, they absorb the moisture in the air and become stale quickly.

MARINADE

2 Tb Five Spice powder
1 tsp minced ginger
1 tsp minced garlic
3 Tb soy sauce
3 Tb sherry

DRESSING

½ cup honey
1 Tb salt
1 tsp pepper
1¼ cup corn oil
¼ cup sesame oil
1 cup rice wine vinegar
1½ tsp dry mustard

OTHER STUFF

2 whole chicken breasts (large), halved
2 heads thinly chopped clean and very dry romaine or iceberg lettuce
½ package rice sticks (3½ oz.)
4 slivered green onions, white part only. Cut them into 2-inch lengths, halved lengthwise, then halved lengthwise again.
¾ cup finely chopped toasted cashews (these must be chopped by hand)
3 Tb toasted sesame seeds
8 sprigs cilantro

Step 1: Marinate the chicken

Mix together all the ingredients for the marinade and place in a plastic bag with the chicken breasts. Tightly seal the top and shake bag to thoroughly coat breasts. Refrigerate overnight, making sure the marinade covers all the chicken.

Step 2: Cook the chicken and the skin

Bake at 375 degrees for 45 minutes, then turn oven to 450 degrees for another 10 minutes. Brush chicken breasts with marinade several times during the baking. Remove from oven and let cool for 15 minutes. Remove the skin and place it in a pan. Bake the skin for 20 minutes at 375 degrees, until very crispy and dark brown. Cool, then place in the bowl of a food processor fitted with the steel S-blade and process until ground thoroughly. Set aside.

Step 3: Cut the chicken

Remove meat from bones, cool, and with a sharp knife cut against the grain into bite-sized strips. Toss with skin.

Step 4: Make the dressing

Mix all the ingredients together either briskly with a whisk or in the bowl of a food processor.

Step 5: Fry the rice sticks

Heat 6 cups corn oil over medium heat in a 6-quart pan that's at least 6 inches deep until a tiny piece of rice stick explodes when dropped into the oil. Break rice sticks in half lengthwise; place half of the rice sticks into the oil; they will puff instantly. Remove with a large slotted spoon immediately and drain on paper towels. Repeat. It's important to fry the noodles as close to serving time as possible. Do not overcrowd the oil; the rice sticks expand enormously.

Step 6: Assemble

In one bowl, toss lettuce with about ⅔ of the dressing. In another, mix the chicken and cashews with remaining dressing. Place lettuce on plates, leaving a border around the outer edge of the plate, about 1 inch. Put a nest of noodles on lettuce, then dressed chicken and cashews. Sprinkle sesame seeds along edge of lettuce and green onions on top. Garnish with cilantro. This dish is lovely with an edible flower as another garnish—for example a nasturtium or borage.

MAYONNAISE

It's so easy to make mayonnaise, I can't understand why anyone with a food processor would ever go out to buy it. It can be made with any kind of vinegar you want, including tarragon, rice, raspberry, or sherry wine vinegar, or with lemon juice. For a Chinese Chicken Salad sandwich, make the mayonnaise with rice vinegar and use half corn oil and half sesame oil.

¼ cup vinegar
½ tsp salt
2 tsp Dijon mustard

2 whole eggs
2 cups corn oil

In the bowl of a food processor fitted with a steel S-blade, or in a blender, place ¼ cup of the oil and all the other ingredients. Blend. With the motor continuing to run, add the remaining oil slowly in a thin stream. Mayonnaise mixture will thicken by the time the last drop of oil is added, or a few seconds thereafter.

SALAD DRESSING

My sister, Emily, thinks restaurant cooking is far too chaotic, but she loves to prepare food, and this salad dressing is one of her inventions. Mendocino Mustard is a hot and sweet product. If you cannot find it, use any good Dijon style mustard. The other exotic ingredients in the recipe can be found in markets with a good foreign foods section, or in stores specializing in Oriental foods.

1 cup olive oil
¼ cup rice vinegar
1 bay leaf
1 clove minced garlic
2 tsp Mendocino Mustard or Dijon mustard

½ tsp tamari soy sauce
¼ tsp toasted sesame oil
2 Tb tahini
3 drops Tabasco sauce
piece of peeled ginger the size of a marble

Put everything in a jar with a tight-fitting lid and shake like crazy.

BLACK BEAN MARINADE

Makes about 5 cups

These beans have a very pleasant flavor. They're especially nice on salads. We have to soak the black beans overnight for this one, unlike the Black Bean Chili, for instance. When you soak beans overnight, that's frequently because you want them to look nicer. A marinade is right there on top of the salad, so you want the beans to look right.

The black beans are also known as "black turtle beans"—at least that's what it says on the bags I buy.

2½ cups black beans, sorted (watch out for pebbles)
12 cups water
1 onion, studded with 6 cloves
6 Tb vinegar (either red wine or sherry wine type)

¾ cup olive oil
1 Tb Worcestershire sauce
2 tsp salt
½ tsp black pepper
2 cloves garlic, minced (optional)

Rinse beans and cover with 12 cups of water. Let soak overnight. Add onion, bring to a boil, reduce heat, and simmer for 1½ hours, or until beans are neither crunchy nor sludgy, just firm.

Drain and remove onion.

Make marinade by whisking together vinegar, oil, Worcestershire sauce, salt, pepper, and optional garlic. Pour over hot beans and refrigerate up to 2 weeks.

Stir occasionally. Remove from refrigerator 2 hours before serving. Sprinkle on a green salad.

GARLIC-FLAVORED OIL, PLUS AN EASY WAY TO PEEL GARLIC

If I perform no other service to humanity for the rest of my life, just sharing this secret will no doubt insure my immortality. I've never seen this technique described anywhere, but it is one of the truly great kitchen tips of all time. Eat your heart out, Heloise.

The one important thing to remember is that the garlic cloves need to be heated in the oil for as short a time as possible, using just enough oil to cover them. You can gently stir the cloves around in the oil.

1 bulb of garlic   1 cup olive oil

Slice off the stem of the garlic bulb, and separate the bulb into cloves. Heat olive oil to 230 degrees, turn off heat, and add garlic. After 15 seconds, test to see if garlic is easy to peel by trying it with one clove. It should easily pop out of its skin. Drain and peel all the garlic. Return peeled garlic to cooled oil and store in a covered container. Use oil in cooking or for salad dressings.

Entrées

POLLO DEL SOL

Serves 4

I made this up one night, when someone asked me to give them an original recipe. I just sat around thinking, "What do I feel like cooking, and what ingredients do I have on hand." This is the result, and it's a very satisfying one. Simple, inexpensive, and tasty. (I served this to my friends the Kroningers. I sometimes think of their place as my test kitchen.)

1 chicken, cut into 8 serving pieces
3 Tb olive oil
4 cloves minced garlic
1 onion, finely chopped
¾ cup dry white wine

1 small lemon, thinly sliced, seeds removed
12 Italian dried olives
4 sun-dried or oven-dried tomatoes (see page 167), slivered.

Step 1. Prepare the chicken pieces

Blot chicken pieces with paper towels until they are dry. Heat olive oil in a large skillet. When the oil is very hot, but not smoking, sauté the pieces of chicken skin side down. Sauté for 10 minutes on one side, then 5 minutes on the other side. Remove chicken from skillet, and set aside.

Step 2. Prepare vegetables

Using the same oil in the skillet, cook the garlic and onions over medium heat for 5 minutes, or until the onions are tender. Over high heat, add the wine and all chicken parts except the breast. Add salt and pepper to taste, cover, and simmer for 15 minutes. After 15 minutes, turn chicken pieces over and add breasts, lemon slices, tomatoes, and olives. Cover and cook 15 minutes more. Remove chicken from skillet, arrange on platter.

Step 3. Prepare sauce and serve

Turn up heat, and quickly reduce the liquid until it starts to become syrupy. Spoon it and the tomatoes, lemon and olives over the chicken pieces, and serve.

BLACK BEAN CHILI

Serves 8 generously.
Freezes well.

This recipe originated at Greens, a famous vegetarian restaurant in San Francisco, run by the Zen Center. A couple of years ago, Julia Child came up to Mendocino and ate at Cafe Beaujolais. Everyone was just a-twitter. It was on May 13—you remember these things—and I had made several special dishes. I even made a couple of things from her own books. And what did she end up ordering but Black Bean Chili. Of course afterwards, everyone zoomed to the restaurant to ask what Julia Child ate, and for about six weeks after that, we sold nothing but Black Bean Chili.

It's a simple dish to put together: very flavorful, totally vegetarian, and the least expensive entrée on our lunch menu. We serve it with tortillas, and it has melted cheese in it, so it's a vegetarian dish that supplies complete protein. It freezes well, too.

4 cups black beans (also known as black turtle beans)

3 cups canned crushed whole tomatoes

2 large finely chopped yellow onions

1½ cups finely chopped green bell peppers

½ cup olive oil

2 Tb cumin seed

2 Tb Beaujolais Blend Herbs (see page 256) or oregano

1 tsp cayenne pepper

1½ Tb paprika

½ cup finely chopped jalapeño chiles (canned are fine)

2 cloves garlic minced (optional)

1 tsp salt

½ lb. jack or cheddar cheese, grated

½ cup green onions, finely chopped

⅔ cup sour cream

8 sprigs of cilantro (and if you really like cilantro, then 2 Tb more to sprinkle on top)

Sort through the beans and remove the funky ones and the small pebbles. (They're always there. Our prep cook doesn't like doing it either.) Rinse them well. Place in a large pot, and cover with water to several inches above top of beans. Cover and bring to a boil. Reduce heat and cook for 1¾ hours or until tender. You will need to add more water if you start to see the beans.

When the beans are cooked, strain them. Reserve 1 cup of cooking water and add it back to the beans.

Place cumin seed and Beaujolais Blend Herbs or oregano in a small pan and bake in a 325 degree oven for 10 to 12 minutes until the fragrance is toasty.

Sauté onions, green peppers and garlic in oil with cumin seed and herbs, cayenne pepper, paprika, and salt, for 10 minutes or until onions are soft. Add tomatoes and chiles. Add all to the beans and stir.

To serve, place 1 ounce grated cheese, then 1¼ cups hot chili in a heated bowl. Put a spoonful of sour cream on top of the chili. Sprinkle with 1 tablespoon green onions, and place a sprig of cilantro in the sour cream. Optionally, sprinkle about ½ teaspoon chopped cilantro on top.

CHICKEN AND NUT STEW

Serves 4

Combining meat and nuts is much less common in northern climes than it is in the Caribbean or North Africa. This unusual recipe from Anni Amberger demonstrates that the flavors go together happily regardless of one's latitude. The stew is best served over rice.

1 medium-sized (about 2¼ lb.) chicken, cut into serving pieces
1 tsp salt
¼ tsp cayenne pepper
2 Tb olive oil
4 medium-sized onions, chopped
3 cloves garlic, minced

6 medium-sized tomatoes, chopped
2 Tb tomato paste
6 cups Chicken Stock (see page 117)
½ lb. smooth peanut butter, almond butter, or cashew butter

Season chicken with salt and cayenne pepper. Sauté in olive oil with onions and garlic for 15 minutes. Add tomatoes and sauté additional 5 minutes.

Mix nut butter with tomato paste and chicken stock and pour into pan with chicken. Stir constantly for 5 minutes over medium heat. Adjust for seasoning, remove from heat, and serve.

GNOCCHI WITH CHEESE AND HAM

Serves 4 to 5

This indulgent, luxurious, heavenly, and caloric dish was given to me by Robert Reynolds, who has a restaurant in San Francisco called Le Trou. When I met him, he was pastry chef at another restaurant, turning out wonderful things. I think I had six of his desserts one night.

He's a very talented cook, with a special sense of which flavors go with which others. I would serve this gnocchi (pronounced NYO-key) with simple romaine lettuce salad, perhaps garnished with toasted walnuts, and a walnut oil vinaigrette.

1 cup cold water	1 cup heavy cream
½ cup unsalted butter, cut into tablespoon-sized pieces	1 oz. finely chopped flavorful ham (Westphalian, Prosciutto)
1 cup flour	4 oz. flavorful cheese (Muenster, Stilton, Gorgonzola)
½ tsp salt	
3 whole eggs	

Step 1: Start Boiling Water #1

Fill a 6-quart pan ¾ full of water. Bring to a boil.

Step 2: Start Boiling Water #2 to begin making paste

In a medium-sized pan, place the 1 cup cold water and butter, and bring to a boil. The idea is to have the water in this pot come to a boil by the time the butter has completely melted.

Add ½ teaspoon salt to the flour, and add flour to the water all at once. Remove pan from heat and beat madly with a wooden spoon, to make a smooth paste.

Put the pan back on the stove, lower the heat, and dry the paste by scraping it toward you with the wooden spoon or a spatula, flipping the paste over. Keep the paste moving to dehydrate it. The less water remaining, the more readily the paste will absorb the eggs.

The paste will steam, form a film on the bottom of the pan, and butter will glisten on the surface.

Step 3: Add eggs

Remove pan from heat. Add whole eggs one at a time. Each time an egg is added, the paste will appear to separate. Continue beating with a wooden spoon, and it will come back together.

Step 4: Make gnocchi

Put the finished paste in a pastry bag, fitted with the nozzle but no tip. Thus there will be a large hole for the paste to come through. Hold a knife or scissors in one hand, and the pastry bag over Boiling Water #1 in the other. Squeeze and cut after 1 inch of paste emerges. The knife or scissors will get gummy, so occasionally dip this tool in the boiling water and it will cut easier. The dumplings will fall into the water and sink to the bottom. When they rise to the top (in about 30 seconds) they are done. Remove with a slotted spoon to a buttered plate.

Step 5: Bake gnocchi and serve

Heat oven to 325 degrees. Butter a medium-sized 8 × 8-inch baking dish, and pour in enough cream to coat it. Cover with chopped ham, then half the cheese, then the gnocchi, then the remaining cheese, and finally the remaining cream. Turn oven to 300 degrees, and bake for about 1 hour, until cream is absorbed and gnocchi turn golden.

ROAST LEG OF LAMB STUFFED WITH EGGPLANT

I was delighted that Pam Michels sent me this recipe, because she is without a doubt one of the finest cooks I've ever met. She has a good sense of flavors that work well together. Her specialties are foods from Italy or the south of France, of which this method of preparing lamb is a splendid example.

1 leg of lamb (about 4 lbs. with bone, 3½ without), boned and butterflied	1 eggplant, sliced ¼ inch thick
4 cloves garlic, minced	2 red bell peppers
freshly ground pepper	½ cup chopped parsley
1 cup olive oil	sprigs of fresh oregano
juice from 2 lemons, strained	1½ cups white wine
½ onion, chopped	salt
	1 Tb unsalted butter

Mix 2 cloves of garlic, freshly ground pepper and 2 tablespoons olive oil together and rub into surface of meat. Place in a large bowl and pour half the lemon juice over meat, cover, and set aside to marinate, at least 4 hours.

Sauté onion in 2 tablespoons olive oil until soft. Set aside.

Grill or sauté eggplant until partially blackened, brushing it with olive oil as it cooks (about ¾ cup in all). Set aside.

Roast peppers under broiler or over a flame until blackened and place in plastic bag. Close tightly and let sit 10 minutes, then remove skin and seeds. Cut into ½-inch slices and set aside.

Remove meat from marinade. Spread onion and parsley over inside of meat to cover, leaving a 1-inch margin all around. Lay pepper strips over onions, then eggplant slices on top, overlapping if necessary. Salt and pepper.

Roll roast and tie both width- and lengthwise. If filling starts to come out, stuff it back in. Place on a rack in roasting pan. Mix together 2 cloves of garlic, salt, pepper, 2 tablespoons olive oil, and remaining lemon juice. Rub over outside. Tuck in sprigs of oregano.

Roast at 350 degrees, basting with ¼ cup white wine every 15 minutes (a total of 1 cup). Turn roast halfway through to brown evenly. It is done (rare) when internal temperature is about 135 degrees. Let rest 15 minutes.

Pour off pan juices, and remove grease carefully with a spoon. Then pour ½ cup white wine in pan. Place over medium heat and with a whisk, scrape all the bits of meat that are stuck to the bottom. Reduce by half. Meanwhile, untie roast and slice. When the sauce is reduced, whisk in 1 tablespoon butter and pour over meat.

ON AGAIN, OFF AGAIN CHUCK ROAST

Serves 6

When I was growing up, this roast was a definite part of my life. It's the sort of thing my mom used to make in between teaching and gardening and shopping and all. Laura Katz, who, as far as I know invented (or discovered) the technique, has known my mom for years and gave her the recipe ages ago. This is a very simple way to cook meat, and the onions give it an outstanding taste. Even though I don't eat all that much beef nowadays, I love this roast.

2½ to 3 lb. chuck roast, at room temperature
1 tsp salt
freshly ground pepper

3 cloves garlic, minced
2 yellow onions, peeled and thinly sliced

Rub salt, pepper, and garlic into chuck roast, and place in a Dutch oven. Cover with the onions. Cover and place in a 350 degree oven for 1 hour.
   Remove cover and bake for 1 more hour.
   Replace top and bake for 1 more hour.

CHICKEN STUFFED UNDER THE SKIN

Inspired by Richard Olney's recipe in *Simple French Food*, I made a dish even richer than his. In the restaurant, we called it "Chicken Beaujolais" because the staff seemed to grow squeamish calling it by its rightful name, as above.

This dish was so popular, for a while we took it off the menu, because that was all people ever ordered. I would make other wonderful things, but to no avail; customers just wanted this. Many people have asked, "How did you get the stuffing under there?" Well now they're going to find out.

We usually make this with grated zucchini because there's always so much around, but my personal favorite is the eggplant. The mushrooms are nice, too, or you could mix two or more vegetables together.

The recipe may look complicated, but it's really basically simple and straightforward. When it's really busy at the restaurant, we've made as many as 40 servings in one night. You can prepare the chicken in the morning, or the evening before, if you wish, and refrigerate until ready. You can also serve the dish cold, for a picnic or whatever. Sometimes, for a change, I remove and discard the skin from the cooked cold chicken and purée the stuffing and meat or just chop them up finely. A delicious sandwich filling!

1 whole chicken, 2½ to 3 pounds
1 cup finely chopped onions
3 Tb olive oil
1⅓ cups grated vegetables (zucchini, eggplant, mushrooms, or a combination; grate just before using)
4 cloves garlic, minced
½ tsp Beaujolais Blend Herbs (see page 256) or oregano

⅛ tsp finely and freshly ground pepper
12 oz. natural cream cheese or goat cheese (I like California Chèvre), or a combination of the two
1 egg
1 egg yolk
½ cup grated dry cheese (Asiago, Parmesan, dry jack, or a combination)

Step 1: Make cream cheese mixture

In a large bowl of an electric mixer, mix the cream cheese, eggs, and dry cheese together. Set aside.

Step 2: Cook vegetables

Sauté onions in oil over medium heat for 5 minutes, or until translucent. Add grated vegetable(s), garlic, herbs and pepper. Turn up the heat and briskly toss vegetables in pan. The goal here is to keep the vegetables as dry as possible, while cooking until just tender (about 5 to 10 minutes). Scrape the vegetables into a strainer, and let as much liquid as possible drip out. Press occasionally to help the process along. Let drip for about an hour. (Save the liquid for a soup stock.)

Add the vegetable mixture to the cream cheese mixture and blend thoroughly. Refrigerate for 1 hour.

Step 3: Stuff the chicken

Remove the giblets and liver, and any extra fat. With heavy scissors or kitchen shears, cut the backbone completely out, and save for stock. Turn the chicken skin side up with wings closest to you. Break the breastbone by applying pressure (see illustration).

Loosen the skin by slipping your hand between the skin and the flesh, moving your hand gently around the breast.

Put the stuffing mixture in a pastry tube fitted with a big point, and insert the stuffing by placing the point under the skin. You can stuff the breast, thigh, and leg (but not necessarily all the way down the drumstick). Wings cannot be stuffed. Place in a 10 × 15-inch baking pan, skin side up. You can cover the chicken with plastic wrap and refrigerate it at this point, then bake it later in the day.

Step 4: Cook

Bake at 375 degrees for 1 hour and 10 minutes. Let sit 3 to 5 minutes, and cut into 4 servings: 2 of thigh + leg, 2 of breast.

CATALAN BAKED FISH (MERO À LA PASTELERA)

Serves 8

My Catalonian friend, Joana Bryar-Matons, made this at a family dinner we had one winter. It's a real expression of her personality, and of Catalan cooking. She's one of those people who cooks spontaneously; I really had to wrench a formal recipe from her. She serves the fish with white beans, boiled, salted, and drizzled with olive oil. You might think, "Oh, just beans. No big deal." But they were rich and flavorful—a wonderful counterpart to the fish.

The olive oil in the recipe should be virgin or extra virgin, and not some cheap stuff that tastes like it came from a crankcase.

2 lb. filet of red snapper or rock cod, all bones removed
½ tsp salt
½ tsp pepper
1 lemon, quartered lengthwise, then thinly sliced
¼ cup minced parsley
2 Tb dry bread crumbs

2 cloves garlic, minced
⅔ cup chopped almonds
1 tsp paprika
¼ cup olive oil
½ cup tomato sauce
½ cup dry white wine

Brush bottom of a 9 × 13-inch glass baking dish with about 1 tablespoon olive oil. Lay fish filets in the dish to coat, and flip to coat other side. Sprinkle both sides of fish with salt and pepper. Fit into dish, folding under the thin end of the fish. Cover with lemon slices.

Mix together and pat on top the following: parsley, bread crumbs, garlic, almonds, paprika and olive oil. When patting onto fish, leave a margin of 1 inch all around the edge.

Mix together tomato sauce and wine and pour over fish. (You can cover and refrigerate overnight at this point. Return to room temperature before baking.) Bake at 425 degrees uncovered for 15 minutes. Do not baste.

MENDOCINO FISH STEW

Serves 4

I tend to like fish prepared in a very simple manner. This is a relatively uncomplicated dish I've been making for years. It's come through several incarnations and now it's a nice meal, on the light side, that goes equally well with potatoes, rice, or noodles.

There aren't many things you can fix with canned tomatoes that come out great. This is one of them, so you can make it even when fresh tomatoes are terrible.

Once you have all the ingredients ready, it takes perhaps 5 to 7 minutes to make this.

2 cups minced red onions
⅓ cup olive oil
2 Tb minced garlic
1½ lbs. fish (snapper or any rock fish) cut into chunks about 1 to 2 inches square
1 cup dry white wine
2 Tb green peppercorns
⅔ cup whole canned tomatoes

⅓ cup pitted green olives with pimientos, sliced
⅓ cup pitted black olives, sliced
4 Tb fresh basil, chopped
cooked rice, red potatoes (cut into quarters or eighths), or noodles
freshly ground black pepper
¼ cup chopped parsley

Sauté onions in olive oil for 5 minutes over medium heat. Add garlic, stirring briefly. Turn up heat, add fish, and toss it around in the pan, so that all sides are partially cooked.

Add white wine and cook for 1 minute, turning pieces of fish. Add peppercorns, tomatoes, and olives, and let simmer for 1 minute. Then add basil, and stir to combine.

In a heated bowl, place rice, potatoes, or noodles, then spoon fish and tomato sauce into each bowl. Grind pepper over top, and sprinkle with parsley.

STUFFED VEAL ROLL

Serves 4

Erich Schmid is the manager of our local bank, the Mendocino branch of the Savings Bank of Mendocino County. In that capacity, he had the the foresight to help the restaurant along during the lean years when life occasionally grew somewhat bumpy. He is also good cook, as evidenced by this recipe of his own creation. It's easy to make, but quite elegant. Be sure that you get real veal, and not the baby beef that is sometimes passed off as veal. When fully cooked, the roll will still be a little pink on the inside, but that's from the Prosciutto, and not because it isn't done.

1 boned breast of veal, about 1½ lbs.	½ cup grated Mozzarella cheese
2 shallots	3 oz. very thinly sliced Prosciutto
½ cup chopped parsley	¼ cup olive oil
½ cup chopped celery leaves	1 Tb fresh rosemary chopped, (or 1 tsp dried rosemary)
salt and pepper	1 cup dry white wine
¼ cup grated Parmesan cheese	1 cup Chicken Broth (see page 117)

Spread out the veal, smooth side down, and pound it with a mallet (if necessary) to make it as even as possible.

In the bowl of a food processor fitted with a steel S-blade, place the shallots, parsley, and celery leaves and chop until the mixture is very fine. Salt and pepper the veal roll and spread this mixture all over it, leaving a 1-inch margin around the edge of the entire piece.

Mix together the two cheeses and sprinkle over the chopped mixture. Lay the Prosciutto over the cheeses. (It is OK if the slices overlap).

Starting with the smaller end, roll up the veal, tucking in loose edges as you go. Tuck the ends into the roll as you form it. Tie the roll firmly with string.

Heat the olive oil in a heavy pot that has a tight lid, and brown the veal roll on all sides. Leaving the meat in the pot, add rosemary and wine, and simmer the liquid until it is reduced by half. Cover the pot tightly and braise very slowly for about 25 minutes, or until the veal reaches an internal temperature of 150 degrees. Check the meat from time to time, rolling it over and basting it with pan juices.

Let cool for 15 minutes. Meanwhile, add chicken stock to the pan and cook down, scraping bits in the pan. Strain and serve with the veal.

ROAST BONED LEG OF LAMB

Serves about 8

We've served this lamb for years in the restaurant. Fresh rosemary is so easy to grow, it's a shame to use anything else.

It is entirely reasonable to ask a butcher to bone the lamb for you, and once that is done, you can produce this dish quickly and easily, and it is superb. Below see the method of rolling and tying the stuffed leg of lamb. I happen to like lamb rare, but of course you can cook it longer if you wish.

1 leg of lamb (about 4 lbs. with bone, 3½ without) boned, trimmed of fat, at room temperature

½ cup unsalted butter, softened

6 cloves garlic

2 Tb fresh rosemary (or 2 tsp dried rosemary)

2 tsp Herbes de Provence, or dried basil and thyme

⅛ tsp freshly and finely ground black pepper

1 cup dry Marsala or Madeira

3 cups Chicken Stock (see page 117)

2 Tb fresh rosemary (or 2 tsp dried rosemary)

¼ tsp black pepper

¼ tsp salt

4 Tb unsalted butter, cut into tea-spoon-sized pieces

In the bowl of a food processor fitted with a steel S-blade, place butter, garlic, rosemary, Herbes de Provence, and pepper. Blend thoroughly. Smear this mixture all over the inside of the leg. Roll and tie the lamb (See illustration). Bake at 375 degrees for about 1 to 1¼ hours. Meat is done (rare) when internal temperature is about 135 degrees. Remove from oven and wrap in foil.

Degrease contents of the baking pan, and place the remaining juices in a pan with Marsala or Madeira, chicken stock, more rosemary, salt, and pepper. Boil over medium heat until reduced by ⅔ and thickened. Strain.

Remove lamb from foil and add strained juices to the reduction. Cut lamb in thin slices. Whisk butter with lamb juice and reduction over medium heat. It will become an emulsion—a thickened sauce. Dribble sauce over lamb, and serve on warmed plates.

BOEUF À L'ORANGE INDIENNE ©

Serves 5 to 6

This recipe was devised by Jay Perkins, who owns a wonderful cooking school called Cordon Rouge in Marin County, California. Jay is an extremely knowledgeable cook. His recipe is a wonderful blending of traditional and unusual flavors. The curry can be pretty intense, but the citrus gives it a certain crispness. It's a nice change from the typical things people do with a beef brisket. It looks complicated, but it's simple to put together, yet exotic enough to serve when entertaining. Because there *are* so many flavors, it may be wise to serve the dish with simple vegetables, and perhaps potatoes.

1 whole fresh brisket of beef (about 3 lbs.)	**SAUCE**
	6 medium oranges
1 cup flour	zest (orange part) of 3 of above oranges
1 tsp salt	about 4 cups of braising liquid from above recipe
¾ tsp freshly ground black pepper	
2 Tb corn oil	½ cup sugar
1½ large onions, sliced	⅓ cup red wine vinegar
4 cups red wine	1 Tb arrowroot
4 cloves garlic, finely chopped	1 Tb curry powder
	2 tsp ground cumin
	1 cup Madeira wine

Wipe both sides of brisket with a damp cloth. Mix together flour, salt and pepper. Dredge with seasoned flour by forcing flour into the meat on both sides with the heel of your hand. Pour oil into roasting pan and heat to very hot but not smoking.

Place the dredged brisket in the pan, fat side down, and sear until it's a rich golden brown. Flip and sear the other side. Remove all oil except a thin layer on the bottom of the pan.

Spread sliced onions over seared meat, then pour red wine over the top of the onions. Lift the brisket so the wine flows under it. Sprinkle minced garlic over the top, and add additional freshly ground pepper.

Place a tight-fitting lid on the roasting pan and bake at 275 degrees for 3 hours, turning every hour.

When tender, remove from pan and wrap in foil.

Pour the braising liquid into a pot (should be about 4 cups), skim to remove fat, and reduce so ⅔ of the original liquid remains.

Combine sugar and red wine vinegar, and carmelize to a medium brown by placing over medium heat for about 5 minutes.

Add reduced stock and simmer for 5 minutes. *Do not boil.*

In a small bowl, combine the arrowroot, curry powder and cumin; with a whisk, blend in the Madeira. Remove stock from heat, whisk in the Madeira-arrowroot mixture, and return to heat. Add orange zest and simmer for 10 minutes.

To serve, slice the beef and place overlapping slices on a warmed platter or individual plates. Divide oranges into segments and place the segments on the meat. Bring sauce almost to a boil and spoon sparingly over meat and oranges.

MARINADE FOR SALMON OR ALBACORE

Makes about 4½ cups

One of my favorite memories is of the summer night a few years ago when Sam Shook, an old friend and talented fisherman, brought pounds of fileted fresh albacore tuna to the Beaujolais as a gift. Heaven-sent! We grilled all of it, and used this delicious marinade, developed by his wife (and our gardener), Desiree Douglass.

⅓ cup brown sugar	2 tsp minced garlic
1½ cups soy sauce	½ tsp black pepper
1 cup water	½ tsp Tabasco sauce
1 Tb minced onion	1½ cups dry white wine

Mix all ingredients together. Marinate salmon steaks or albacore tuna chunks (about 2 inches square) for at least 8 hours, in the refrigerator. Remove from marinade and pat very dry. Grill (over hickory, apple or cherry wood if at all possible) until done. Alternatively, wrap the albacore chunks in bacon, secure with toothpicks, and grill.

TURKEY STUFFING

Enough for a 12–14 pound bird, plus lots of leftovers

Since I moved to Mendocino and found myself in the restaurant business, I've never had the kind of Thanksgiving I remember having as a child. In the midst of Thanksgiving week, the last thing I seem able to do is have a relaxed traditional feast. But last year we decided to do it up right, with the whole family, and I invented a stuffing for the occasion. I used ingredients we had around. (I know most people don't have wild rice around, but it's really necessary for this splendid stuffing). It's an improvisation that turned out just right.

Of course you can use it in a chicken or goose—and there are those of us who just like stuffing as a side dish, never mind the turkey.

You can vary the recipe to your heart's delight. You can put in dried fruits (up to a cup). But basically it's quite complete—everything *I* want to find in a stuffing.

STOCK
turkey neck and gizzard
1 stalk celery, in chunks
½ onion
1 carrot, in chunks

STUFFING
1 onion, minced
8 cloves garlic, minced
2 cups celery, sliced
¼ cup + 3 Tb unsalted butter
3 cups mushrooms, sliced

2 Tb Beaujolais Blend Herbs (or oregano and/or rosemary)
¾ cup parsley, minced
8 oz. water chestnuts, sliced
2 cups cooked wild rice
1 cup pine nuts, toasted
2 tsp salt
¼ tsp black pepper
11 cups day-old cornbread, crumbled
¼ cup turkey stock

Step 1: Prepare turkey stock

Place neck and gizzard in water to cover, with 1 stalk celery in chunks, half onion, and carrot. Simmer for 1 hour. Strain, then reduce liquid to ¼ cup.

Step 2: Make the basic stuffing

Sauté minced onion, garlic, and sliced celery in ¼ cup of the butter for 10 minutes. Add mushrooms and herbs and sauté for 5 more minutes. Transfer to a large bowl and add parsley, water chestnuts, wild rice, pine nuts, salt, pepper, and cornbread.

Add stock, tossing with your hands to thoroughly mix ingredients. The mixture should be only very slightly moist.

Step 3: Stuff the bird

Stuff the bird. Put remaining stuffing in a 9-inch square pan. Cover with aluminum foil, and bake at 325 degrees for 45 to 60 minutes. Drizzle with 3 tablespoons melted butter.

160   CAFE BEAUJOLAIS

Vegetables/Rice

TANGY BEETS

I invited a couple of vegetarian friends to Thanksgiving dinner one year, and then I got terrified that they wouldn't have enough to eat. We served a lot of vegetables that year. I usually prefer my vegetables plain, but I thought the beets could benefit from some sprucing up. Since I had crème fraîche on hand, it occurred to me to add the crème fraîche and mustard to the boiled beets. The sweet flavor of the beets and the strong flavor of the mustard go together beautifully. Ordinarily (except for borscht) I wouldn't think of anything creamy for beets, but there's something about the sharpness and texture of this combination that's delicious.

For each serving:

2 large or 3 small beets

2 tsp whole grain mustard with seeds

4 tsp Crème Fraîche (see page 244) or sour cream

pinch of salt

Slice off the ends of the beets and boil until tender—about 30 minutes. Cool, then remove skin with a small paring knife. Cut into slices, and then cut each slice into matchsticks.

Mix together mustard and crème fraîche. Add to the beets and gently heat.

CAULIFLOWER OR BRUSSELS SPROUTS

This recipe should really be called "Vegetable," as if it were one chapter in a three-page generic cookbook: *Meat, Vegetable, Dessert*. It's just a different, and very satisfactory way of preparing either of these vegetables, neither of which is among the world's most popular.

The technique for preparing them is one of those things that's so easy to demonstrate, but so hard to describe in writing. You want to shave off cauliflower crumbs as if you were whittling it. You can grate the brussels sprouts on a grater, but it's hard not to grate your knuckles too. A food processor does a better, or at least a safer job on them.

Brussels sprouts, when grated, are like a whole new vegetable. Many people can't identify them, other than to guess that they're in the cabbage family. The flavor seems to come out more, too. With either vegetable, it's an easy dish to make, fast, and inexpensive, too.

2½ cups cauliflower, whittled into crumbs, as described above, *or*
2½ cups grated brussels sprouts, as described above
2 Tb unsalted butter

¼ tsp salt
2 pinches white pepper
1 Tb lemon juice, strained
3 Tb Parmesan cheese (optional)

At medium high heat, melt butter in pan, and when foamy, add cauliflower or brussels sprouts, salt, pepper and lemon juice. Toss vegetables around with a flick of the wrist, or use a spatula. Immediately turn heat down to low. Place a tight-fitting lid on pan and steam for 2 minutes. Taste. If too crunchy, replace lid for 1 more minute. When as tender as you wish, serve as is, or add Parmesan cheese.

LEEKS IN MUSTARD CREAM

When I asked Kathi Wentzel, a talented artist who lives in Amsterdam, for some typical Dutch dishes I might try in the restaurant, I recoiled in horror at her suggestions. Are we really ready for Belgian endive with bananas? But this leek dish sounded good, and turned out to be excellent, and easy for the American palate to appreciate.

6 large leeks with a green core to
    the end; use all the white part
    and about 4 inches of the green,
    cleaned carefully as described
    below. Cut into 1-inch pieces.
¾ cup heavy cream

2 Tb Dijon mustard
1 tsp fresh dill weed
1 tsp salt
¼ tsp white pepper
2 Tb chopped parsley

The really important thing about leeks is to clean them thoroughly. Sand and dirt are trapped inside. Slice the root end off not far up the white part. Make a crossed incision in the bulb part. Leave about 4 inches of the green part on, and soak to allow the dirt to come out.

    Steam leeks until tender, but not soggy for about 5 minutes in a basket apparatus suspended over a pot of boiling water, so that the water doesn't touch the bottom of the basket. Drain exceedingly well. Whip cream with mustard, dill weed, salt, and pepper until thickened but not stiff. Toss leeks in mustard cream. Garnish with parsley and serve immediately.

WHITE BEAN GOOP

*Serves 8 as a side dish;
also a soup base*

I didn't know what else to call this. This is what I call it in my own recipe book, so why not here. It *is* a goop—a very buttery mixture. The beans we use are called Great Northern white beans. The cooked beans become saucy and delicious, with the help of their own starch. You can serve it with lamb. Or you can use it as the base of a soup. (For soup, mix this recipe with 8 cups of chicken stock and purée. Serve with crème fraîche as a garnish.)

It's nice to try to cook beans just right. At first they're crunchy, and eventually they get kind of sludgy. We want them in between, when they're soft but not sludgy. Some people become complacent when they're cooking beans—how can you overcook a bean, they think—and then they've boiled them so long, the beans are practically turned inside out.

12 cups water
3 Tb olive oil
1 Tb salt
2⅓ cups Great Northern white beans
2 tsp dried tarragon or 4 tsp fresh tarragon
⅔ cup chopped parsley

10 cloves garlic, peeled
8 shallots, peeled
1 tsp salt
1 tsp white pepper
⅓ cup unsalted butter
3 Tb lemon juice
⅔ cup Crème Fraîche (see page 244)

Heat water, olive oil, and 1 tablespoon salt to boiling and add beans. Bring to boil again and boil 2 minutes uncovered. Remove from heat, cover, and let sit for 1 hour. Then simmer until soft but not sludgy. This will take up to 2 hours.

Blend tarragon, parsley, garlic, shallots, 1 teaspoon salt, and pepper in the bowl of a food processor fitted with a steel S-blade. Cook the mixed blend in butter for 1 minute, and remove from heat. Add lemon juice and crème fraîche; combine with cooked white beans. Adjust for seasoning. Keep warm in the top of a double boiler.

POTATO GOOP

Serves 8

We're only including two goops in the book. They're so very rich, and in general, I try to limit my production (and intake) of that stuff. But they're also so good. The Cholesterol Advisory Board especially loves this one. It's their *raison d'être*.

Potato Goop is a variation on the theme of garlic and butter and olive oil. You just smear it on cooked potatoes and bake them, and they get crunchy and crusty. It's very heavily herbed and spiced—and remarkably good. When one is left in the kitchen at the restuarant late at night after a long day, one could put away quite a lot of this. It's been done.

3 lbs. small red potatoes, unpeeled

½ cup unsalted butter, melted

¾ tsp salt

⅓ cup olive oil

3 cloves garlic, peeled

4 shallots, peeled

½ cup chopped parsley

⅛ tsp black pepper, freshly and finely ground

Early in the day, parboil the potatoes until just tender, and refrigerate.

Melt butter. Place salt, olive oil, garlic, shallots, parsley and pepper in the bowl of a food processor, and blend until thoroughly combined, using a steel S-blade. Pour into another container and stir in melted butter.

Cut the potatoes into quarters and place on a 9 × 13-inch pan. Add the goop, mixing the potatoes with your hands, and spread the potatoes out on the pan in a single layer. They should be covered with goop on all sides. Bake at 350 degrees for 2 hours, until crispy. Stir periodically.

VERY BAKED TOMATOES

This is a recipe that came about because during the summer, I am quite uncontrollable when it comes to ordering tomatoes. They are one of my favorite vegetables (or fruits, if you want to be fussy). The fog belt ends about two miles east of Mendocino, and the people who live inland can grow things we can't grow right on the coast. Tomatoes happen to be one of them.

A friend made a version of these—in Italian, they are called burned tomatoes, because they cook so long. What happens is that the tomatoes collapse; all of the water is exuded. They look awful, but they taste terrific. Then, since, of course, I can't leave well enough alone, not only do I bake them in olive oil, I add the garlic and basil. The flavor is so intense. If you love tomatoes, those will be a real treat. Nothing else has this flavor. You serve these leathery things as a side dish with lamb or other entrées. It works especially well with ripe tomatoes, particularly the Roma variety. The natural sweetness is accentuated, and the slight leatheriness makes an interesting texture. I've eaten as many as five of these at a sitting. Dangerous.

Make this recipe in conjunction with something else that needs to be baked.

4 tomatoes, the riper the better, in season, and preferably home-grown	4 cloves garlic, peeled and minced
¼ cup olive oil	2 Tb chopped fresh basil or 1 Tb chopped fresh rosemary
	salt and pepper

Core tomatoes. Slice in half horizontally—across the middle, not through the core, and place in a baking pan, cut side up. Mix together oil, garlic, basil or rosemary, salt and pepper. Pour over the 8 halves.

Bake at 325 degrees for 2 hours. The tomatoes will exude their juices and collapse, and then begin to caramelize. *This* is when they start to become delicious.

Remove tomatoes from pan using a slotted spoon and serve.

OVEN-DRIED TOMATOES

I have commented in about 28 other places how wonderful sun-dried tomatoes are. But the last time I checked, they were going for over $20 a pound in the Berkeley gourmet ghetto. Jane Benet, food editor for the *San Francisco Chronicle*, performed a tremendous service for humanity when she created this homemade version and put it in the newspaper. I actually prefer these to sun-dried tomatoes, if the truth be known. They're almost prune-like (which is good!). Since tomatoes are technically a fruit, I toyed with the idea of using them in a dessert but have never gotten very far with that idea. If you do, write me.

5 lbs. Roma (Italian-style) tomatoes	salt olive oil

Select firm tomatoes. Cut a ¼ inch slice from the stem end of each tomato. Cut each tomato nearly in half lengthwise, leaving it attached at the opposite end, and opening flat so the cut sides are exposed.

Place on cake racks, cut side up, not quite touching each other, and place the racks on baking sheets. Sprinkle the cut surfaces of tomatoes with salt, then place in a 200 degree oven, and dry for about 8 hours if you have a gas oven. Using an electric oven, you can bake the tomatoes for 6 hours in the afternoon, turn off the oven, and leave them in overnight. In the morning, turn the oven to 200 degrees and bake for one more hour. They are ready when they have shriveled, and feel dry. (They should be slightly flexible, not brittle.)

Pack in a jar (or jars), and cover completely with an excellent-quality olive oil. Put a lid on the jar, and store in a dark place for 4 weeks before using.

Yield: about ½ cup of dried tomatoes from each pound of fresh ones.

ARMENIAN RICE PILAF

This dish is almost obscenely rich, but thankfully you don't realize that while you're eating. I've never met Helen Jenanyan, my friend Gary's mother, but I've had the opportunity to taste her rice pilaf on enough occasions to know it belongs in this book. It's an authentic Armenian recipe.

4 cups Chicken Stock (see page 117)

8 oz. unsalted butter, cut into table-spoon-sized pieces

1½ tsp salt

freshly ground black pepper

3 Tb safflower or other light oil

1⅓ cups loosely packed vermicelli broken into 1 to 1½-inch pieces

2 cups long grain white rice

½ cup toasted pine nuts or blanched unsalted almonds (optional)

Put butter and chicken stock into a 2-quart saucepan. Add 5 or 6 grinds of black pepper and the salt. Bring to a boil. If boiling occurs before next step is completed, cover and reduce heat. It must be boiled again before proceeding.

In a heavy-bottomed 3- to 4-quart casserole, heat the oil until hot. Add vermicelli, stirring rapidly and constantly until light gold in color. Add the rice, stirring constantly. Continue to stir the mixture until most of the rice grains have turned from dull white to slightly translucent, with a bright white center. The vermicelli should be uniformly golden. This entire process should take 5 or 6 minutes if the heat is right.

Remove from heat. Very slowly, with your face well away from the casserole, pour the boiling stock/butter mixture over the rice/vermicelli mixture. Return to stove and adjust the heat to the lowest possible setting. Cover tightly and let simmer for 25 minutes.

Slide cover slightly off the casserole and let cook for 10 more minutes. Do not stir the rice or the pilaf will become mushy and broken. Look at the pilaf. The vermicelli should be beginning to curl. Let rest for 15 more minutes. Correct seasoning if necessary.

If you wish, gently fold in toasted pine nuts or blanched unsalted almonds.

Breads

Here are eight important considerations in making any yeast-based bread, in addition to the instructions for each particular recipe.

1. Beating

Development of the gluten ensures a fine crumb. This is accomplished by sufficient beating and kneading of the batter. The batter should be beaten thoroughly after half the flour has been added. Finished dough should be kneaded for a full 5 minutes after all the flour has been added.

2. Kneading

Dough loves to be handled. One of the biggest problems people have is being timid about touching the dough. Knead it, hit it, throw it on the table. Dough thrives on abuse.

3. Timing yourself

Five minutes is a lot longer than you think, if you are kneading dough with appropriate vigor. Time yourself.

4. Rising

Make certain that your yeast is not past the expiration date shown on the packet. Use no yeast after its time. Never be in a hurry when you want to make bread, and never add extra yeast to speed it up. It will take about 4 hours to turn out a batch. Plan your schedule accordingly. A second rising in the bowl always gives a finer crumb.

5. Adding more flour

If you've kneaded and added flour, and are reluctant to add more for fear of adding too much, cover the dough with a dry towel and leave it alone for 5 minutes. Wash your hands and dry them thoroughly, and return to the dough. Try the technique described in number 6. Nine out of 10 times, the dough will no longer be sticky, or tacky. Don't ask me why—I just know that this works, and I have saved a lot of bread from unneeded extra flour.

6. Testing for done-ness

To determine if dough does need more flour after kneading, place your clean dry hand on the dough for 5 seconds, then remove it slowly. It should feel only slightly tacky, not sticky. If your hand sticks to the dough, then add a little more flour. Too much flour means a dry, heavy bread, and why go to all the trouble for that.

7. *How to knead*

With the dough in front of you, place your hands on top of dough. Press into the dough with the heels of your hands, using a forward rolling movement. Then pull dough back toward you with a quarter turn. The dough lifts and turns. Continue these motions without pausing after the turn. Knead continuously. This rhythm is not tiring, and enables you to knead for a long time.

8. *Forming loaves*

Divide dough into as many parts as there will be loaves. Pat each piece into a 7 × 10-inch rectangle. Roll up tightly. The ends of the dough should touch the ends of the pan. The dough will lengthen as you roll it. The seam should be on the bottom. Do not press the dough down or alter the rounded top after it is in the loaf pan.

CHALLAH (EGG BREAD)

Makes 2 loaves, braided or plain

This is a traditional Jewish egg bread that I've been making since I was a teenager. It's probably the most satisfying bread I've ever made because it's such a responsive dough—bouncy and easy to work with. There are many different interpretations of challah—it's a great all-around bread.

If you're feeling adventurous, you can make one giant loaf instead of 2 smaller ones. Take about ¾ of the dough to make the 3 large ropes for the braid. Divide the remaining quarter into 3 parts and make an identical baby braid to put on the top, or make a coiled braid from 2 ropes. Be sure to fasten the ends together and tuck them under. It's very impressive to behold.

In any event, see the generic bread instructions on page 169 as well.

2 Tb dry yeast
1½ cups warm water
2 Tb sugar
2 tsp salt

2½ Tb corn oil
3 eggs, beaten
about 5 cups white flour
3 Tb poppy or sesame seeds

Mix together yeast, ½ cup warm water, and sugar in a small bowl. Set aside in a warm place for 5 minutes.

In a larger bowl, whisk together 1 cup warm water, salt, corn oil, 2 eggs, yeast mixture, and 2½ cups flour. Beat until elastic (about 5 minutes). Exchange a heavy wooden spoon for the whisk and gradually beat in about 2¼ cups more flour, working flour into dough vigorously.

Turn out onto a *very* lightly floured surface and knead until smooth and elastic (about 5 minutes). If dough appears to need more flour, read the general introduction, part 6 first.

Put dough in a greased bowl and turn it over to grease the top. Cover with plastic wrap and a towel, and let rise in a warm place until doubled in size (about 1 hour).

Punch down, turn out and knead for 1 minute to get rid of air bubbles.

For braided bread
Divide dough into 6 equal parts. Roll dough into ropes of equal length, about 15 inches long, and make 2 braids of 3 strands each. For the most uniform shape, start from the center and braid to one end. Secure the ends and tuck them under, then turn the unbraided ends toward yourself and braid them in reverse of the other side. Place each on a 10 × 15-inch greased cookie sheet.

For loaves
Divide dough in half. Form each portion into a ball, then roll out until they are long enough to touch the edges of an 8 × 4-inch loaf pan. Place in 2 greased loaf pans. Do not press the dough down or alter the rounded top in any way.

Cover loaves or braids with a dish towel and let rise 45 minutes or until very light. Brush with beaten egg, dipping the brush into the egg lightly and brushing it on the dough from the pan up. (Don't get egg on the pan or it will bake onto the pan and be difficult to remove.)

Sprinkle with seeds and bake for 30 to 35 minutes at 375 degrees. Check after 20 minutes. If the bread is getting too brown, cover with a piece of foil.

To bake in loaf pans, grease 2 9 × 5 inch pans and shape each ball into logs long enough so that the dough touches the ends of the pan.

HERB BREAD

Makes 2 loaves

When I was in my teens, my parents took my sister and me to a wonderful cafeteria in the Bay Area where this delicious herb bread was served. The owner graciously gave me the recipe which I've adapted somewhat. We serve it at dinner from time to time, for toast and for sandwiches, especially Croque Beaujolais (see page 186). The dough is green, but the finished bread doesn't end up that way.

When I make bread, I use a whisk for the first half of the stirring in of the flour, because it effectively beats the developing batter into a smooth mass. The second half can be done with the traditional wooden spoon.

See also the general essay on bread on page 169.

2 Tb yeast	⅓ cup fresh parsley, chopped and packed
1½ cup warm water	2 tsp dill weed
6 Tb sugar	1 tsp dill seed
2 eggs	1 cup onions, finely chopped
⅓ cup corn oil	up to 7 cups white flour
2 tsp salt	melted butter
1 tsp anise seed	

Dissolve yeast in warm water with sugar. Stir briefly and place in a warm spot for 5 minutes. In a large mixing bowl, place eggs, oil, salt, parsley, anise seed, dill weed, and dill seed, and whisk together. Check the yeast mixture. It should be bubbling and look lively. If not, check the expiration date on the yeast. Maybe you need to get fresh yeast and try again. Stir yeast mixture and add to the large bowl.

With a whisk, add 3 cups of flour gradually, and beat vigorously for 5 minutes, scraping down sides from time to time. You will start to see elastic threads form around the inside of the bowl.

Replace whisk with a strong wooden spoon. Add the chopped onion. Gradually add 3 more cups of flour, making certain after each cup that the flour is thoroughly absorbed.

Turn out dough onto a lightly floured board and knead, using ½ to 1 cup more flour. This dough always feels slightly damp, so be careful with the amount of flour added. Total kneading time is 5 minutes past the last addition of flour. It will help if you lightly butter your hands before kneading.

Put dough into a greased bowl, turn to grease top, and cover bowl tightly with a piece of plastic wrap. Cover again with a dish towel, and place in a warm place to rise until doubled in size, which should take about 2 hours. Punch down, and knead for about 30 seconds to remove air bubbles. Divide in half, and form into loaves.

Place in 2 well-greased 8 × 4-inch bread pans. Cover with dish towel, and let rise in a warm place until doubled, which should take about 1 to 1½ hours.

Butter the tops with a little melted butter and bake at 375 degrees for 30 minutes, or until a rich golden brown. Remove from pans and let cool.

CHEESE-AND-WINE BREAD

Makes 2 loaves

I made up this recipe years ago when I was working at The Cheese Shop in Mendocino. I wanted something that showed off both cheese and wine. If you use the large amount of (optional) garlic, you might wish to retitle the recipe "Cheese-Wine-and-Garlic Bread."

After a while at the restaurant, you feel as if you've made every kind of sandwich under the sun, so the only thing left is to come up with new bread. We use this one often; it has evolved into a great basis for a large number of recipes. A roast beef sandwich on Cheese-and-Wine Bread is just fantastic. We do it with homemade mayonnaise, mustard, lettuce, tomatoes, and onions. It's delicious with sun-dried tomatoes which I mention elsewhere (see page 167). We also serve an open-faced vegetable sandwich: tomatoes, lettuce, sprouts if you can stand them, and grated carrots.

See the generic bread instructions on page 169 as well.

6 Tb unsalted butter	1½ cups dry white wine
6 Tb finely minced garlic (optional)	2 eggs, beaten
½ cup minced green onions	1 tsp salt
2 pkgs. dry yeast	6 to 6½ cups flour
4 tsp sugar	1 lb. aged Asiago or dry jack cheese,
¼ cup warm water	cut into ½-inch cubes

Step 1: Cook onions (and optional garlic)

Sauté onions (and optional garlic) in butter for about 30 seconds, without permitting them to burn. Set aside and cool.

Step 2: Make yeast mixture

Dissolve yeast and sugar in water. Stir and set in warm place for 5 minutes. Mixture should be bubbly. (If it isn't, your yeast may be too old. Check the expiration date on the package, and if it was too old, discard and try again. Better still, check the date before you start.) Stir again.

Step 3: Make dough

In a large bowl, whisk together wine, eggs, salt, and yeast mixture. Gradually add 3 cups flour, and beat for about 3 minutes until elastic threads start to form around edge of bowl. Add cooled garlic and onion mixture, and with a large sturdy wood spoon, beat in 2½ to 3 cups more flour.

Turn dough out on a very lightly floured board, and knead until smooth and springy. (It's OK if it's slightly tacky.) Cover with a clean dry dish towel and let rest 5 minutes. Knead again. Dough should *not* be tacky at this point; if it is, add ¼ cup flour and knead 5 more minutes. (You should *always* knead for 5 minutes after adding flour.)

Step 4: Let dough rise

Place dough in a large greased bowl, turn so it's greased all over, and seal airtight with plastic wrap. Put in a warm place and let rise until doubled— about 1 hour. Punch down, turn out, and knead a few times to pop air bubbles.

Step 5: Add cheese and let rise again

Divide dough in half and knead half the cheese into each piece, forming 2 balls. If you wish to bake these free form, place on a lightly greased baking sheet, and press to flatten slightly. (You can also form them into whatever shape you want—oblong, baguette, etc. Just remember the dough is heavy because of the cheese, so it's not as flexible in shaping.) Put in a warm place, cover with a dish towel and let rise until almost doubled, about 45–60 minutes.

To bake in loaf pans, grease two 9 × 5-inch pans and shape each ball into logs long enough so that the dough touches the ends of the pan.

Step 6: Bake

Preheat oven to 375 degrees, and bake for 25 minutes. Reverse pans (top to bottom, back to front) and bake for another 5 to 15 minutes. (Loaves in 9 × 5-inch pans will take longer than free form loaves). Check by tapping on bottom. They should sound hollow when done.

Remove loaves from pan and cool on wire racks for at least ½ hour before slicing.

CRUNCHY WHEAT BREAD

You wouldn't think that adding rye flour would make a bread so special, but it came to me to try it, and I just love the way it tastes. This has become my favorite wheat bread. It seems strange to some people to add nonfat dry milk solids. If you add liquid milk, it has the effect of making the bread more tender. If you add dry solids, it gives the breadcrust a crisper texture.

2 Tb dry yeast	8 Tb butter, melted, or corn oil
½ cup hot water	up to 4½ cups white flour
½ cup honey or barley malt syrup	¾ cup whole wheat flour
½ cup nonfat dry milk solids	¾ cup rye flour
1¾ cups milk, warmed	¾ cup cracked wheat
2½ tsp salt	½ cup wheat germ

In a small bowl, mix together hot water and honey or syrup. When just warm to the touch, sprinkle yeast over surface, stir twice, and set in a warm place for 5 minutes. The yeast will become foamy. Stir to mix, and pour into a large bowl. Whisk in milk solids, milk, salt, and 6 tablespoons of melted butter or corn oil.

Add 4 cups white flour and whisk vigorously for 5 minutes. (You may wish to time yourself—5 minutes is longer than most whiskers think.) Mix together whole wheat and rye flours, cracked wheat, and wheat germ.

Replace whisk with a heavy wooden spoon and gradually beat in the whole grain flours and about ¼ cup white flour. Turn out onto a very lightly floured board and knead. Add more flour if necessary (but read instruction on page 169). Knead for 5 minutes.

Place in a large greased bowl. Turn over once (now the top is greased) and cover tightly with plastic wrap and a dish towel. Let rise in a warm place until doubled, about 1¼ hours. Punch down, cover, and let rise again until doubled (about 1 hour). This second rising is not essential, but it produces a finer crumb.

Punch down, turn out, and knead a few times. Divide in half, shape into loaves, and place in 2 greased 8 × 4-inch loaf pans. Cover with a dish towel and let rise until doubled (about 45 minutes).

Brush tops carefully with remaining melted butter or corn oil, and bake at 350 degrees for 45 minutes.

RACHEL'S PUMPKIN MUFFINS

*Makes about
30 muffins*

My clientele is nuts about this. We don't make these too often, but when we do, we make 12 dozen at a time, and we usually sell out in one day. Rachel Katz made these for me when I was down at Santa Cruz years ago. They're spicy, kind of dense, but not too heavy. We serve them warm, with butter. They're really substantial. They're great for church bake sales and other fund-raising-type activities (like running a restaurant!).

2 cups brown sugar	1 tsp nutmeg
1 cup corn oil	1 tsp allspice
4 eggs, beaten	1 tsp cinnamon
1 lb. canned pumpkin	½ tsp cloves, powdered
3½ cups flour	⅔ cup water
2 tsp baking soda	½ cup chopped walnuts
2 tsp salt	½ cup raisins
1 tsp baking powder	

Mix together sugar, oil, eggs, and pumpkin. Sift together all dry ingredients, and add, a little at a time, alternating with water, to the pumpkin mixture. Beat after each addition. Rub walnuts lightly in large metal sieve to remove skins. Stir in the walnuts and raisins.

Place muffin papers in muffin tins, and fill ⅔ full. Bake at 350 degrees for 25 to 30 minutes.

BRAN MUFFINS

Makes about 3 dozen muffins.

This is a really down-to-earth bran muffin recipe. The only problem is that these muffins stick to those damn papers, and we've never figured out a way to have them not stick. (We'll send a dozen Congo Bars to the first person who sends us a non-stick method that works. Decision of the judges is final.) They're not too sweet, and they smell really great while they're cooking. Some of us even think they smell better than they taste. When I'm upstairs working, I'll come downstairs to the kitchen and say, "What's that wonderful smell?" It's become a joke by now. The staff points out that this is the umpteenth time I've come down with that question—and that I don't even like to *eat* the muffins that much. But they sure do smell great.

One nice thing about this recipe is that the batter holds, and you can keep it in your refrigerator for up to a week, perhaps longer.

1½ cups 100% bran cereal	¼ cup raisins or other dried fruit
½ cup very hot water	⅓ cup light brown sugar
1 cup buttermilk	1¼ cups flour
1 beaten egg	2 tsp baking soda, sifted
¼ cup corn oil	¼ tsp salt

In a mixing bowl, combine bran and water. Add buttermilk, egg, oil, and raisins. Blend.

Then add the sugar, flour, baking soda, and salt. Mix thoroughly. Fill muffin papers ⅔ full, and bake at 350 degrees for 25 to 30 minutes.

The batter can keep for a week or more in the refrigerator in a tightly covered container. Before using, stir to distribute the fruit.

ZUCCHINI MUFFINS

About 12 muffins

In Mendocino, we always have an excess of zucchinis in the summer, and we try to use them as creatively as we can—as in this nice little muffin. They're sweet, but not overly so. Serve them for breakfast, warm with butter.

2 eggs	½ cup sugar
7 Tb corn oil	1¾ tsp cinnamon
1½ tsp lemon juice	¾ tsp baking soda
grated rind of 1 lemon	¾ tsp baking powder
1 tsp pure vanilla extract	½ tsp salt
1 cup grated zucchini	⅓ cup chopped walnuts, toasted
1 cup + 6 Tb flour	

In a large bowl, mix together eggs, oil, juice, rind, and vanilla. Add zucchini and stir.

In a separate bowl, sift together flour, sugar, cinnamon, baking soda, baking powder, and salt. Add to zucchini mixture, and stir well. Rub walnuts lightly in large metal sieve to remove skin then add walnuts to batter. Fill muffin papers ⅔ full. Bake for 30 to 35 minutes at 350 degrees.

WHIPPING CREAM BISCUITS

I'm crazy about breadstuff in general, and biscuits in particular, and these biscuits from Kathi Riley most of all. They are *so* rich, and yet they are absolutely the lightest biscuits I've ever seen in my whole life. The procedure is a standard one, but the ingredients are special: butter and heavy cream throughout, and you can really tell the difference. They rise very high. They're very impressive, and great at breakfast.

Be sure to cut them out as close together as possible, so you won't have to reroll the dough. Rerolling makes the dough tougher, and the biscuits heavier. Alternatively, make square biscuits.

In the restaurant, we serve these for Sunday breakfast along with Chicken-Apple Sausages (see page 200) and scrambled eggs.

1½ tsp sugar	¼ cup unsalted butter, cut into ½
2 cups white flour	teaspoon-sized pieces and frozen
1 Tb baking powder	1 cup + 2 Tb heavy cream
1 tsp salt	

Mix dry ingredients together. Add butter, and blend either with an electric mixer or briskly with your fingertips, rubbing the dry ingredients with the butter until the butter is broken up into smaller pieces (about the size of peas).

Add heavy cream, and combine all ingredients with a fork until just moistened. Immediately turn out on a lightly-floured board, and knead about 10 times. It's OK that small lumps of butter are visible.

Roll out to ¾ inch thickness and cut with a floured cutter, 2 inches in diameter, as close together as possible to minimize rerolling, or make square biscuits. Layer the leftover bits and pieces, knead together 2 or 3 times, pat out dough again, and cut out biscuit rounds again.

Place biscuits on an ungreased cake sheet and bake at 425 degrees for 15 minutes, or until golden brown.

Breakfasts/Light Meals

OMELETTES

Eggs. It's a wonder I still eat them after all the contact I've had. I added it up, and last year, Cafe Beaujolais turned approximately 111,600 eggs into omelettes and scrambled eggs. Here is how we cook them.

With a fork, beat together 2 eggs, 1 teaspoon cold water, and 2 drops of Tabasco sauce until blended. Do *not* use a machine or an eggbeater to do this.

Heat the pan. (I prefer SilverStone pans because they prevent sticking and enable you to use less butter.) Add 2 teaspoons unsalted butter, or a mixture of butter and oil, or oil. Butter will foam. When it subsides, pour in eggs. Let them cook about 5 seconds, then grab the pan handle and start to swirl the egg mixture in the pan.

With a wooden spatula, pull the outside toward the center, tilting the pan to allow uncooked egg to spill into the pan.

When eggs appear to be a cohesive mass, you can either flip them, or fill them with whatever filling you had in mind and serve. Unflipped eggs are easier and less prone to disaster, and also come out creamier. I flip eggs because I find most people prefer them slightly more cooked.

On Flipping Eggs

Pick the pan up and, with a sharp jerk forward, flip the eggs. Then immediately fill them with whatever, and turn onto a warmed plate. Flipping is not that hard, but it takes practice to learn. When you jerk your arm forward and up, the eggs flip almost automatically because of the arc formed. To practice, flip a flat omelette over and over and over again in the privacy of your kitchen. Don't worry about making a mistake. Your dog or cat will love it, even if it's leathery by the time they get it. It's best to practice in private. Friends and family seem to enjoy making fun of people during their flipping apprenticeship, and, since you will inevitably make many mistakes, do it alone.

OMELETTE FILLINGS

Here are seven of my favorite omelette fillings. Each recipe is sufficient for a 2-egg omelette, so adjust quantities as needed. Creativity in substitution of ingredients is encouraged.

SAUTÉED HAM AND APPLE WITH BRIE

½ cup unpeeled diced (½-inch cubes) apple (Pippins are good)
2 tsp unsalted butter
2 oz. diced ham

a pinch of Beaujolais Blend herbs (see page 256) or oregano
3 Tb dry white wine
1½ oz. Brie cut into a thin strip

Sauté apple in butter with herbs over medium heat for 1 minute. Add ham and continue sautéing for 1 minute. Add white wine and reduce until liquid is syrupy. Place Brie in center of omelette and add ham and apples. Fold in half and serve.

SMOKED SALMON *or* HERBED CREAM CHEESE

3 Tb Smoked Salmon Filling (see page 188) or Herbed Cream Cheese (see page 189)

1 small potato, in ½-inch cubes
2 Tb unsalted butter
¼ cup chopped tomatoes (optional)

Boil potato and let it cool. Cut into eighths and sauté in butter until crispy. Spread filling in a strip on half the omelette, add potatoes and optional tomatoes, fold in half, and serve.

GREEK OMELETTE

2 Tb green onions, chopped
2 oz. feta cheese, crumbled
¼ cup tomatoes, diced, or 5 cherry tomatoes, halved

1 cup fresh spinach leaves (optional), steamed or quickly sautéed
3 Greek olives

Toss green onions into hot butter when preparing omelette. Sprinkle feta in omelette. Add tomatoes and optional spinach, fold in half, garnish with olives, and serve.

GLORIFIED SWISS CHEESE OMELETTE

2 Tb walnuts, chopped and toasted
2 Tb finely chopped green onions
1/4 cup Swiss cheese, grated
1 strip bacon, fried and crumbled

1 Tb sour cream
1 red potato, boiled, cooled, and cut into eighths
1 Tb unsalted butter
1 clove garlic, minced

Rub walnuts lightly in large metal sieve to remove skins. Mix together walnuts, green onions, Swiss cheese and bacon. Sauté potato in butter until crispy. During last minute or two, add the garlic. To fill omelette, place walnut mixture on one side, spread sour cream over, add potatoes, fold, and serve.

OLÉ OMELETTE

1/4 cup Black Bean Chili (see page 144)
3 Tb grated jack or cheddar cheese
2 Tb mashed avocado

1 Tb sour cream
1 Tb salsa—high-quality commercial is OK

Place chili in a strip on one side of the omelette. Sprinkle cheese on chili. Mix together avocado, sour cream and salsa, and spread over cheese. Fold in half and serve.

CHILDHOOD FAVORITE

2 Tb cream cheese

2 Tb raspberry jam

Dot the cream cheese on half the omelette. Repeat with jam. Fold and serve with a toasted bagel.

CRISPY CHEESE OMELETTE

1/4 cup croutons (consider Herb Bread, as on page 172)

1/4 cup cheese of your choice, grated

Arrange croutons over half of omelette. Sprinkle cheese over croutons. Fold in half and serve.

SWEET PEPPER AND GARLIC OMELETTE

This is a part of my continuing salute to garlic. I devised it following a request from a friend who was writing a magazine article on garlic. This was during the summer when we had wonderful green, yellow, and red peppers from local gardens, and local basil. You can put almost anything you want in the omelette as a filling. This version is very satisfying as a vegetarian dish—or you can add Italian sausage. Not many people seem to know about Kasseri cheese, but it's one of my favorites.

3 cups bell peppers, thinly sliced (ideally a combination of red, yellow and green; if not, then 2 cups red, 1 green)

3 Tb olive oil

3 Tb garlic, finely minced

2 Tb fresh basil, chopped

¼ tsp salt

⅛ tsp finely and freshly ground pepper

8 eggs

2 Tb cold water

9 drops Tabasco

2 Tb olive oil

2 Tb unsalted butter, melted together with the olive oil

½ cup grated Parmesan cheese

½ cup grated dry jack or Kasseri cheese

Heat the olive oil in a sauté pan until hot, and add peppers. Cook 4 minutes, or until just tender. Add garlic, basil, salt, and pepper, and combine. Cover and reduce heat. Cook for 2 minutes. Keep warm.

Whisk together eggs, water, and Tabasco. (See page 181 for specific omelette instructions.) Heat an 8-inch omelette pan, and add 1 tablespoon of the oil/melted butter combination.

When butter foams, add ¼ of the beaten eggs, then follow omelette instructions. Fill omelette with ¼ of cheese, then ¼ of sautéed peppers. Make 3 more omelettes.

EGGS BEAUJ-OLÉ

This is a version of a recipe that Pam Hahn, local sculptor and artist, gave me years ago. It's a sort of Mexican-like not-quite-an-omelette. What I like about it is the same thing I like about putting potatoes in omelettes: people aren't used to these combinations, but they're so good. The tortilla adds nice flavor and texture. Think of it as egg helper. Meal in a skillet. Especially good served with crispy fries and sour cream.

1 corn tortilla

corn oil for frying (the amount will depend on how many chips you are making and how you make them. For one tortilla, you can use as little as 3 tablespoons of oil, and flip the chips around as they cook to insure heating on all sides. Or you can use an inch of oil and "deep fry" them.)

2 tsp butter

1 Tb minced green onion

2 eggs, beaten with 2 tsp water

1 Tb mashed avocado

1 Tb salsa—high-quality commercial is OK

Cut the tortilla into 20 pieces by making 3 cuts one way and 4 cuts the other way.

Heat corn oil in a deep pot until very hot but not smoking. Drop one piece of tortilla into the oil. The tortilla will sizzle when the temperature is right. Dump all the pieces in at once and keep the heat medium high. (Stir once if you're using the deep fry method; constantly if you're using minimal oil.) After 30 seconds, check a chip. When it is crunchy, remove all from the oil with a slotted spoon and drain on a paper towel. Salt lightly.

In a pan, melt butter, and when bubbling, add green onions. Stir for 30 seconds, then add crisp tortilla chips. Throw in eggs. Scramble and turn out onto a warmed plate. Place avocado and salsa in the center.

CROQUE BEAUJOLAIS

Makes 4 sandwiches

This evolved from a traditional French sandwich called Croque Monsieur. It has more of a tang than the usual croque does. At the restaurant, we've been making it on our own Herb Bread (see page 172), which makes it very special.

8 oz. Swiss cheese grated
½ cup Crème Fraîche (see page 244)
2 Tb Dijon mustard
¾ cup milk
3 eggs

1 pinch salt
1 pinch ground white pepper
⅛ tsp nutmeg
8 slices day-old bread
4 slices ready-to-eat ham
½ cup unsalted butter

Mix cheese, crème fraîche, and mustard together and set aside.

Whisk together milk, eggs, salt, pepper, and nutmeg. Dip bread into mixture until it is soaked but not soggy. Quickly brown ham slices on both sides, and set aside. (The fat of the ham is sufficient; no other fat needed.)

You will have to decide how many sandwiches to make at once, depending on the size of pan. For each sandwich, sauté 2 slices of bread in 1 tablespoon butter until golden brown on one side. Flip and add another tablespoon butter.

On 1 of these slices, place ¼ of the cheese mixture and a sautéed ham slice. Cover the pan (containing both slices) with a lid until the cheese melts—about 3 to 5 minutes. To serve, make a sandwich by covering the melted cheese with the other sautéed slice of bread.

CRÊPES

This is my favorite of many recipes for crêpes. We've made countless thousands of them. I make them in my 8-inch SilverStone pan—the same one I use for omelettes. It works beautifully, heats evenly, and doesn't stick. I don't find those specialized crêpe pans especially useful. I make crêpes *in* the pan, the way we were meant to.

There are, of course, any number of fillings for crêpes. You might consider Herbed Cream Cheese (see page 189) or Smoked Salmon Filling (page 188).

Even though the recipe is very clear, you may have to adjust it as you go. Flour absorbs differently from batch to batch. If you're having difficulty making thin enough crêpes, it's probably because the batter is too thick, or perhaps the pan has cooled off or gotten too hot. By the time you've made your first 20 or 30, you'll have it down pat, and be ready for our kitchen, where one person tends 4 pans at once. It's like learning to ride a bike. Once you've got it, you'll never lose it.

6 eggs	6 Tb corn oil
1⅔ cups milk	2 cups flour
1 cup water	melted unsalted butter
½ tsp salt	(for greasing pan)

Mix all ingredients except butter together in a blender for 30 seconds. Strain through a sieve into a container. Cover and refrigerate for at least 2 hours before using.

When ready to prepare crêpes, stir the batter. The first 2 or 3 are experimental; the batter may need to be thinned with a few drops of water.

Heat an 8-inch SilverStone pan over medium heat until a drop of water flicked on the surface jumps around. Grease lightly with melted butter using a pastry brush, and pour about 3 teaspoons batter into the pan, tilting it in all directions so that the batter is even on the surface. If there's an excess of batter, pour it into the bowl. Crêpes are very thin—about 1/32-inch thick.

Cook until the edge of crêpe is lightly browned (about 45 seconds). Loosen with a spatula (wood or plastic if you're using SilverStone), and use your fingers to grab the edge and flip it over. Cook for about 20 to 30 seconds and slide out of pan onto a plate. Repeat, stacking crêpes.

Package tightly and refrigerate for up to 3 days. To keep longer, freeze. Allow frozen crêpes to come to room temperature in the refrigerator before using.

SMOKED SALMON FILLING

This filling can be used as a sandwich spread or to fill omelettes, crêpes, or bagels. Cream puffs if you're adventurous. Possibly best when licked off the ends of your fingers.

I usually use belly lox, but I have used dried smoked salmon made locally at Noyo Harbor. It's tangier, and smokier than delicatessan salmon. Because any smoked salmon is going to be salty, I don't add salt. The filling can be as smooth or as textured as you wish, depending on how long you blend it. I prefer a shorter time, because otherwise you have pink goo. I like to know I'm eating salmon, so I keep it a little chunky. I usually use this filling with sautéed potatoes *inside* the omelette.

5 oz. smoked salmon, chopped coarsely	⅓ cup finely chopped green or red onions
12 oz. natural cream cheese	5 drops Tabasco sauce
8 oz. sour cream	2 Tb heavy cream

Place all ingredients except salmon in the bowl of a food processor fitted with a steel S-blade, or in the bowl of an electric mixer. Blend until smooth. Add the salmon, and mix with a spoon, or blend further if you prefer a smoother consistancy.

HERBED CREAM CHEESE

Makes about 2¾ pounds

This is an all-purpose item that can be used equally well in omelettes, as a dip, on sandwiches, accompanying raw vegetables, etc. You can use the herb mixture without the cream cheese to flavor mayonnaise. You can use good goat cheese in place of, or in addition to the natural cream cheese.

We serve an herbed cream cheese omelette at the restaurant, and it's equally popular at breakfast and at lunch.

3 Tb chopped chives
3 Tb chopped parsley
4 Tb chopped green onions (white and green sections)
4 large cloves garlic, peeled
1½ Tb vinegar (I prefer tarragon vinegar)

¼ tsp freshly and finely ground black pepper
2½ lbs. natural cream cheese or fresh goat cheese, or a combination of the two

Place all ingredients except cream cheese into the bowl of a food processor fitted with a steel S-blade. Process for 15 seconds. Place cheese in the bowl of an electric mixer. Add the herb mixture and beat thoroughly. The finished product lasts about a week in the refrigerator.

A tablespoon of the herb mixture alone (no cream cheese) can be added to ½ cup mayonnaise for use on sandwiches or hamburgers.

SPICY BUTTERMILK COFFEE CAKE

This is our famous coffee cake. We have actually tried to stop making it, but our customers refuse to let us. They say, "This is like the coffee cake I grew up with!" Our poor prep cooks are very, very tired of it, but it will probably go on forever. It's an old-fashioned sort of cake. For a generation that purports to be as health-conscious as ours, it's got everything going against it. But people eat more of this cake than you would believe. Our waitresses find it addictive, too. It does taste wholesome.

It's easy to whip together. You can make the first part the night before, and then finish it up in the morning, and have a fresh, warm cake for breakfast or brunch.

2¼ cups flour	¾ cup corn oil
½ tsp salt	1 cup chopped walnuts or pecans
2 tsp cinnamon	1 tsp baking soda
¼ tsp ginger	1 tsp baking powder
1 cup brown sugar	1 egg, beaten
¾ cup white sugar	1 cup buttermilk

Step 1: Make the batter and topping mix

Mix together in a large bowl the flour, salt, 1 teaspoon of the cinnamon, ginger, both sugars, and corn oil. Remove ¾ cup of this mixture, and to it add walnuts or pecans and an additional 1 teaspoon cinnamon. Mix well, and set aside.

Step 2: Complete the batter

To the remaining batter, add baking soda, baking powder, egg, and buttermilk. Mix to combine all ingredients. (Small lumps in the batter are OK.)

Step 3: Bake

Pour batter into a well-greased 9 × 13 × 2-inch pan. Sprinkle the topping mixture evenly over the surface. Bake at 350 degrees for 40 to 45 minutes.

FRENCH TOAST

Serves 4 to 5

I've been making this since since I was nine years old. My father, who is quite an aficionado, likes it just as much now as he did then. You can use any kind of bread. I use baguettes, brioche, wheat, white, raisin bread, almost anything. When we make it with baguettes at the restaurant, we call it Silver Dollar French Toast. To me, it is the epitome of special breakfast stuff. We use real maple syrup, of course, and give you enough so you can have maple syrup soup if you insist. I hate those little "individual portions" of maploid syrup you get in so many places. I recommend a brisk walk after eating this.

28 slices baguette
   (cut on the diagonal) *or*
12 slices day-old bread
   (white, wheat, raisin brioche)
4 eggs

⅔ cup milk
½ tsp cinnamon
½ tsp vanilla
4 Tb unsalted butter

Beat together the eggs, milk, cinnamon, and vanilla. Dip slices of bread in mixture until soaked through, but not soggy. Be sure the bread is not dry in the middle.

In a large (10-inch) frying pan, melt butter over medium heat. Add bread, fitting the slices in comfortably next to one another. Sauté until richly browned (about 5 minutes), then flip, adding more butter, and continue to sauté until both sides are identical.

Serve with powdered sugar and real maple syrup or your favorite jam.

A DELICIOUS SYRUP

Makes 3 to 3½ cups

This is my variation of a recipe introduced to me by my friend Mary Ellen Black. It's just great with waffles, pancakes, and ice cream. The barley malt syrup has a deep rich flavor and, combining it with butter gives it a creamy texture. If you've ever thought, "I would like a syrup to be richer," then this is that syrup.

½ to 1 cup chopped toasted
   walnuts
½ cup unsalted butter, melted

¾ cup maple syrup
1½ cups barley malt syrup

Mix all ingredients together.

SOUR CREAM WAFFLES

Important disclaimer: These are *not* our famous waffles. Our famous waffles are *not* going into this book. I've had people say, "I can't wait till the book comes out. Those waffles!" Sorry folks. We *might* consider it in the sequel. Instead, you get our second most famous waffles. Some people actually like them better. They're a totally different kind of waffle from our famous ones. I experimented with many waffles when we got our new waffle machine last year, and these were the best newcomers. They're crisp, and they have a good flavor.

They're fine plain, or you can put in toasted nuts, wild rice, bacon, or sautéed apples. This is a perfectly respectable waffle recipe, even if it is not the one you wanted to know.

2 cups white flour
2½ tsp baking powder
¾ tsp baking soda
½ tsp salt
1 Tb + 1½ tsp sugar
4 eggs, separated

1 cup sour cream
1½ cup milk
¾ cup + 2 Tb melted unsalted butter, corn oil, or a combination of the two

Sift together all dry ingredients. In a separate bowl, beat together the egg yolks, sour cream, milk, and melted butter. Add to the dry mix. Mix together thoroughly. Beat egg whites until stiff, and fold in completely. Make waffles the way you usually do. (If you usually don't, follow the waffle iron instructions.)

Variations to add to waffle batter: a) 1 cup chopped nuts; b) 1 cup cooked wild rice; c) 1 cup chopped sautéed bacon; d) sautéed apples made from 2 peeled sliced apples, 2 tablespoons unsalted butter, ¼ teaspoon cinnamon, and 1 tablespoon brown sugar. Sauté apples in melted butter for 2 to 3 minutes. Add cinnamon and brown sugar. Cover and cook on low heat for 2 to 3 minutes. Cool and mix into waffle batter.

RICOTTA PANCAKES

Makes 16 3-inch pancakes; enough for 4 to 5

These light and fluffy pancakes are a recipe from my mom that has really caught on in the restaurant, and in my own life. Many may disagree with me, but I think they taste better without syrup—just with some melted butter. You must understand that I have nothing whatever against syrup. We buy pure maple syrup from Canada, and we go through a 5-gallon pail every week! I love excuses for eating maple syrup, but ricotta pancakes are not necessarily one of them.

4 eggs, separated	2 pinches salt
1 cup ricotta	1½ tsp baking powder
⅓ cup cottage cheese, small curd	¾ cup milk
⅔ cup white flour	

With an electric mixer, mix together all the ingredients except the egg whites until thoroughly blended. Beat egg whites until stiff but not dry, and fold into mixture.

Pour enough batter on a greased griddle to form a 3-inch pancake. Let it cook until bubbles pop on the top—about 1½ minutes. (There will only be a few bubbles—not the many that are typical of regular pancakes.) Flip and cook another 1¼ minutes, until golden brown. Do not press down on the pancakes to "speed up" the cooking. They don't like it; they have to take their own sweet time. (This is also true of hamburgers, by the way.)

If you make the batter ahead of time, keep it in the refrigerator until the moment it is used; this will keep the pancakes from deflating. Do not make batter more than 6 hours ahead of time for best results.

BLUEBERRY CORNMEAL PANCAKES

Makes 18 pancakes

I love to make these, because it's the kind of dish people expect to eat when they come to Cafe Beaujolais. We use a lot of luxury items in our cooking. And we have access to berries from our purveyors, so I like to throw them into things whenever I can. These pancakes are light, not leaden, and they're very attractive. The sort of thing people like to wake up to.

Really the most important thing is the basic technique for making any kind of pancakes. You pour about ¼ cup of batter onto a hot griddle, and cook until bubbles form and start to pop on the top. Flip the pancakes with a wide spatula and brown the other side. The two really important things are just flip them once, and don't smash them down with the spatula in order to brown them. They're just little things; they won't be improved by being sat on.

You can use frozen blueberries. Add them partially defrosted; the heat and steam will thaw them. You can also use huckleberries. You can even use no berries at all.

1¼ cups flour	2 cups buttermilk
1 tsp baking powder	3 egg yolks
3½ Tb sugar	3 Tb unsalted butter, melted
½ Tb baking soda	3 egg whites
½ tsp salt	1 cup blueberries (fresh or frozen)
1 cup cornmeal	

Sift together all dry ingredients. Mix together buttermilk, egg yolks, and butter with dry ingredients. Beat egg whites until stiff but not dry, and fold into the batter.

Pour ¼ cup batter onto hot griddle, sprinkle about 2 tablespoons blueberries on each pancake, and cook until bubbles form and start popping on top. Flip with wide spatula and brown the other side. Turn them only once, and please don't press down on them to accelerate the browning process.

POTATO PANCAKES WITH APPLESAUCE

Makes 24 to 30 pancakes

Jim Katz is the supreme potato pancake maker of all time, as this recipe of his demonstrates. It shows the potato off so well, in terms of flavor and crispness. They can be held at 250 degrees for up to 15 minutes by placing on paper towels in a pan with paper towels on top. (Serve with applesauce, homemade—recipe follows—or otherwise. An entirely satisfactory "otherwise"—a recipe enhancing store-bought applesauce—also follows.)

6 medium-sized red potatoes	½ cup + 2 Tb corn oil
½ small onion	pinch salt
1 egg, beaten	

Peel and grate potatoes, using a large hand grater. Grate the onion. Beat eggs with 2 tablespoons of corn oil and salt. Combine with potatoes and onions.

Pour enough corn oil into sauté pan to cover bottom with about ¹⁄₁₆ inch of oil. Heat to very hot but not smoking, and drop potato mixture into oil by heaping tablespoons. Immediately flatten them out, so the pancakes are about 4 inches in diameter. Smaller sizes will burn. Try to keep them neatly round. Fry until golden brown, flip, and brown other side.

Drain on paper towels.

Serve with applesauce and sour cream.

HOMEMADE APPLESAUCE

4 green apples cut into eighths (not peeled, cored, or seeded)	2½ cups apple juice

Simmer apples in apple juice for ½ hour or until very soft. Drain, reserving the liquid. Push apple through sieve, and discard peel and seeds. Simmer liquid and reduce by half and stir into applesauce.

OTHERWISE

Buy unsweetened applesauce and coarse-grate a peeled apple into it.

FRIED POLENTA

I grew up with this dish, and we always called it "fried mush." But somehow, when I put it on the menu at the restaurant as Fried Mush, people would not order it. I took that personally. Then, for some reason, it became trendy to serve polenta, so that's what we call it, and people order it. My little fantasy is that when someone orders "The Fried Polenta, please," the waitress turns to the kitchen and yells, "Fry one mush."

Polenta is a coarse grained cornmeal. That's all it is. You could actually make this with ordinary cornmeal, but it doesn't have the interesting texture. Essentially what you do is make a stiff cooked cereal, chill it to make it firm, slice it, and fry it.

What I especially like about this is that it's versatile. You have the choice of serving it for breakfast with maple syrup, or as a base for some tomato or pasta-type sauce. You could even make scrapple by adding cooked pork sausage and herbs, and serving it with biscuits and eggs. It's really cheap to prepare, and very satisfying. Quintessential down-home cooking.

5 cups water	2 Tb unsalted butter
1 tsp salt	½ cup cornmeal
1⅔ cups polenta (coarse grain cornmeal)	½ cup unsalted butter

Boil water with salt. Slowly sprinkle in polenta, stirring constantly. Reduce heat and continue stirring. After 15 minutes, the mixture will be very thick. Add 2 tablespoons of butter and stir in. Pour into a buttered loaf pan (8 × 4 × 3 inches). Refrigerate overnight, or at least 8 hours, covered with plastic wrap.

Dip pan into a larger pan of hot water for a few seconds, or into hot water in the sink. Using a knife, gently loosen the sides and invert onto a flat surface. Remove pan. Slice loaf into ½-inch thick pieces, and dredge in dry cornmeal. Melt butter in pan and when hot, add slices. Cook over medium heat for 10 minutes, or until golden brown. Flip and repeat.

Serve with maple syrup for breakfast, or with tomato sauce, melted cheese and sausage for lunch.

FRIED MATZO

This is Jewish French toast. It's really more like scrambled eggs with matzo, but fried matzo is what my grandmother calls it (I have it every morning when I visit her in Los Angeles), and that's what I call it, too.

Like rice pudding, it's the sort of thing many people grew up with, and then somehow forgot how good it was, so they don't have it as adults. I have some reluctance about serving it in the restaurant, because it's, well, messy-looking. It's this great sloppy plateful you'd probably only want to eat at home.

There are two schools of thought: those who eat it plain or with more seasoning (I don't use salt and pepper with scrambled eggs, but I do with fried matzo), and those who eat it with strawberry jam.

    1 matzo   1 Tb milk
    2 eggs   1 cup boiling water
    4 pinches salt   2 tsp butter or corn oil
    2 pinches freshly ground pepper

Beat together eggs, salt, pepper, and milk until all ingredients are combined. Break matzo into 5 pieces and place in a bowl. Add boiling water, wait 3 seconds, and pour water and matzo into a strainer. Add strained matzo to eggs and gently mix together.

Melt butter in a pan over high heat, and add egg-matzo mixture. Cook quickly and, stirring with a wooden spatula, scrape egg and flip uncooked parts so everything is completely cooked and not creamy. Serve with strawberry jam or more salt and pepper.

GRANDMA IDA'S NOODLE KUGEL

You'll either love this or you'll hate it. Maybe to love it, you had to have grown up with a Jewish grandmother nearby. Kugel is an essential part of every Jewish grandmother's repertoire—a creative way to get as many calories into you as possible.

Kugel means pudding, but not in the pudding and pie filling sense. It is starchy, and hearty. The noodles are definable, as in lasagna.

This is a sweet kugel. I eat it for breakfast or for lunch, usually warm.

KUGEL

1 12 oz. package of wide noodles, cooked and drained

16 oz. sour cream and maybe a little more for dollops

16 oz. cottage cheese

¼ tsp salt

1 cup raisins

6 eggs, beaten

grated peel of 1 lemon

⅓ cup sugar

TOPPING

2 cups bread crumbs

¼ cup unsalted butter

3 Tb sugar

1 tsp cinnamon

Place noodles in a large bowl. Add all other kugel ingredients and mix well. You may wish to adjust the quantity of sugar, according to your own taste. Place in 9 × 13-inch baking dish. Cover with plastic wrap and refrigerate overnight.

About 1½ hours before serving, brown bread crumbs in frying pan with butter for about 10 minutes, stirring frequently to avoid over-browning. Add sugar and cinnamon to bread crumbs. Sprinkle topping evenly over top of kugel, and bake for 1 hour at 350 degrees.

Remove from oven, let stand 15 minutes before serving. Serve with a dollop of sour cream.

CORN FRITTERS

Emeline Malpas, who lives in Little River, about three miles south of Mendocino, rediscovered the Early American corn grater—an ingenious scientific instrument that removes precisely that part of the corn that gets stuck in your teeth. The delicious part passes through the grater. You just drop it on the griddle, and make the best corn-flavored stuff you've ever tasted.

Emeline used to sell reproduction corn graters by mail, and the odds are high that she will again. See page 256 for details.

The sugar in corn begins to turn into starch as soon as it is picked, so whenever possible, use corn that was picked within the last two hours. I look forward to the fall each year for just that reason; we do have wonderful corn up here. But these fritters are entirely satisfactory with slightly older corn as well.

2 cups freshly grated corn
2 eggs, lightly beaten
2 Tb flour

1 tsp baking powder
1 tsp salt
ground pepper

Mix all ingredients together. Drop the batter by the generous tablespoon into a very lightly greased nonstick pan. Cook like pancakes, about 1 minute each side, turning once when lightly brown. They are delicious served with sour cream, chutney, or salsa, or with maple syrup or honey.

CHICKEN-APPLE SAUSAGES

Well maybe in the Midwest where pigs are big, you can get things like chicken-apple sausages. But you surely can't around here, except at The Wurst Place, a tiny sausage factory and store in Yountville, California, about an hour's drive north of San Francisco. If you're unable to make the pilgrimage (I do it every few months, myself), then this recipe will work all right with any good pork sausage. (It's better than boiling them to death in water.) But chicken-apple sausage! Worth the trip. Even if you're coming from Parsippany, New Jersey.

Any of the suggested poaching liquids give the sausage more complexity, a sweetness. You can even use flat champagne.

1 cup white wine, champagne, or apple cider

8 chicken-apple sausages
1 Tb butter

Place sausages and wine, champagne or cider in a large skillet. Bring to a boil. Reduce heat and poach sausages for 10 minutes, turning occasionally. Drain. (You can save the poaching liquid and add it in when making a chicken stock.) Then sauté the poached sausages in butter until browned.

SUZANNE'S FAMOUS CASHEW GRANOLA

*Makes 7 cups
without raisins*

Suzanne McKinley is the librarian at the Mendocino Middle School. She worked at the restaurant years ago, and created this recipe. I'm so pleased with it, it's still on the menu with that title. Sometimes we make it with almonds instead of, or in addition to cashews. I used to think granola was the carrot cake of breakfast cereals. Who needs it. But even *I* eat this granola. It's not too sweet. It tastes wholesome, and we don't stint on the expensive stuff, so it's more than a mouthful of oats.

4 cups regular (not instant or quick-cooking) oats

⅔ cup wheat germ

⅔ cup unsweetened big flake coconut

6 Tb sesame seeds

6 Tb sunflower seeds

½ cup cashews, raw, in pieces, or sliced almonds, or both

⅔ cup corn oil

⅓ cup honey

1 tsp vanilla

¼ tsp salt

½ cup dried fruit and/or raisins (optional)

Mix together oats, wheat germ, coconut, sesame seeds, sunflower seeds, and nuts in a large bowl.

In a saucepan, combine corn oil, honey, vanilla, and salt. Cook over low heat until honey is melted. Pour over the dry mixture and blend thoroughly.

Spread out in a lightly greased 10 × 15 × 1-inch pan and bake at 300 degrees for 35 to 45 minutes, stirring every 10 minutes.

Cool thoroughly, add optional fruit or raisins, and store in plastic bag or airtight container.

Serve with fresh fruit and milk.

TRE FROMAGGI SAUCE

Enough for 5 to 6 first courses or 3 to 4 entrées

This means "three cheeses" and it's another one of those extremely indulgent pasta sauces that I advise people to eat as an appetizer rather than as an entrée, because it's so rich. There's no fiber in it. Not one thing that gives you a breather. It's just melted goo, and you put it on pasta, and it *is* good.

You can use different cheeses. I've used Gorgonzola to replace the Parmesan, for instance. But it is the sort of sauce you probably have to go out and buy the ingredients for, as contrasted with the kind of sauce you throw together from what you have on hand. That makes it special. We serve it on fresh pasta.

¼ cup unsalted butter
1 cup heavy cream
3 oz. grated Gruyère cheese

4 oz. grated Parmesan cheese
3 oz. grated Asiago cheese

In the top of a double boiler, place butter and whipping cream, and heat over barely simmering water. When the butter has melted, add the three cheeses, and stir to blend. *Do not let the water boil*. Use immediately.

SUMMER BERRY SOUP

This is a recipe from Sally Koch. She came in one day with berries she had picked in her own yard, the way people do in Mendocinoland, and whipped up this incredibly delicious soup. She had seen a recipe for something like it somewhere—but of course she put her own touch on it. We kept dipping our spoons in and saying, "What do you think." A little of this, a little of that, it just emerged. It has a really intense flavor and a gorgeous sort of purply color. It will work with supermarket-type berries if they're good and fresh. The soup is really very simple to make, and it's one of those happy dishes where the total is much more than the sum of its parts. At the restaurant, we serve it as an à la carte dish on the brunch menu. You could start a nice lunch with it, or even use it as a dessert.

3 cups fresh berries (straw, logan, rasp, or whatever is in season; all one kind or assorted)

½ cup sugar

¾ cup sour cream

¾ cup heavy cream

2¼ cups water

¾ cup light red wine (gamay beaujolais, Zinfandel, or almost any generic red)

dollop of sour cream

sprig of mint

Place berries and sugar in a blender, and purée. Add all other ingredients to the blender and blend. Chill, then serve in chilled bowls with a dollop of sour cream and a sprig of mint.

FRUIT COMPOTE

Makes 8 cups

This is something I grew up with. My mom has been making it all my life. What's curious about dishes like this is that when I try to serve them at the restaurant, they don't go over very well. I suspect it may be the name. I mean, I had something called "Poached Fruit" at an elegant restaurant which turned out to be just poached prunes. My mother's is really much better, I think. It has the tang of oranges and lemons, and you can make it with almost any kind of red or white wine, or sweet or dry vermouth. It's impossible to ruin this recipe.

Save the juice. In fact, this can be a long-lasting compote, if you add fruit from time to time. (Check this out in a wonderful little book called *Instant Gold*, a novel in which Trevisan Fundador's perpetual fruit compote plays an important role in the plot.) My mom sometimes adds thinly sliced raw apple to the cooked compote immediately after removing it from the heat.

1½ cups dried apricots	2 cups apple juice
1½ cups prunes	1 cup water
1 large or 2 small oranges, thinly sliced	5 cloves
1 large or 2 small lemons, thinly sliced	½ tsp nutmeg
	½ tsp cinnamon
3 cups red wine, vermouth (dry or a mixture of dry and sweet), or white wine	¼ cup honey

Combine all ingredients except honey and simmer until fruit is tender, about 30 minutes. Add honey. Cool and refrigerate.

Serve with lightly whipped cream, crème fraîche, sour cream, or over cottage cheese.

Save remaining juice and use in place of apple juice in your next compote, and so on, forever. The juice keeps getting better and better.

Desserts

BUTTERCREAM CARAMEL BARS

This is a great dessert to make in a hurry, although I can't imagine why you would want to adulterate the caramels. You could just eat them plain! Grand Finale Buttercream Caramels are made by my friend Barbara Holzrichter at California's smallest licensed candy factory, in Berkeley—and thankfully, they are available by mail (see page 256). They are soft and creamy and do not stick to your teeth. Supermarket caramels would just walk off the planet if they were confronted by these.

Barbara makes other flavors of caramel—mocha, chocolate, bourbon, etc.—and this recipe will work with them, but buttercream accentuates the butterscotchiness of the recipe.

When I met Barbara years ago, she always carried a pan of caramels, scissors, and cellophane around with her. Everything was wrapped by hand. But then her husband, John, a senior scientist at a big research laboratory, spent five years building an amazing machine, with all manner of mechanical arms and hands that do the packaging semi-automatically. I'm sure Rube Goldberg would have saluted John Holzrichter.

32 Grand Finale Buttercream
  Caramels
½ cup heavy cream
1 cup flour
1½ cups rolled oats
⅔ cup light brown sugar
½ tsp baking soda
¼ tsp salt
¾ cup unsalted butter
1 cup chopped pecans or walnuts

Melt caramels with cream, in a small saucepan over low heat. Stir and set aside to cool. Combine the rest of the ingredients, and press slightly more than half the mixture into a buttered 11 × 7-inch pan. Bake at 350 degrees for 10 minutes.

Remove pan from oven and sprinkle with nuts, then pour over caramel "sauce" and sprinkle remaining crumbly mixture over the top. Bake 15 to 20 minutes longer, until golden brown. Cut into bars after it has cooled.

CONGO BARS

A legend in their own time. These were my first venture into the professional food game. I got the recipe years and years ago, when I was at the University of California in Santa Cruz. When I moved up to Mendocino, I learned that refreshments were needed at the movies being shown at the Art Center. I wanted to do something simple, because I had a full-time job. The Congo Bars could be done in my closet-sized kitchen. I would run home, whip them up, dash over to the movies and sell them. They were warm and full of gooey chocolate chips, and people just flipped over them. So I sold them at every possible Art Center function. Someone (I don't remember who) made up my slogan: "Don't deny that jungle beat, Congo Bars are good to eat."

Even after I owned the restaurant—stepped up, you might say—people would stop me on the street and say, "Aren't you the Congo Bar lady?"

They're just great cookies, and easy to make. You can serve them underneath vanilla (or even chocolate) ice cream, or just rough it and eat them plain. Even people who try not to eat sugar give in and eat Congo Bars. They are best warm, but they're not so bad cold either.

⅔ cup unsalted butter, melted and
   cooled
1 lb. light brown sugar
3 eggs
2¾ cups flour

2½ tsp baking powder
½ tsp salt
1 cup (6 oz.) real chocolate chips
1 cup chopped walnuts

Mix together butter, brown sugar, and eggs, to blend. Mix together flour, baking powder, and salt, and add to first mix. Then add chocolate chips and walnuts. Spread in a well-greased 10 × 15 × 1-inch pan. (This dough is very sticky, so you may have to pat it out.) Bake at 325 degrees for 35 minutes. It will still look soft. Remove and place pan on rack. Cut while warm into 25 pieces.

CORNMEAL GINGER COOKIES

Makes about 55 cookies

This recipe came from my friend, John Carroll. I met him several years ago when I was running a program at the Beaujolais called Great Cooks of California. He has since gone on to do impressive things in the world of professional cooking.

These are thin, crisp, spicy refrigerator cookies with a hint of lemon and ginger—not one of those cookies you can eat and not think about. Cornmeal is an unusual addition, that gives them a little nubbliness. It has a nice juxtaposition of flavors. Once formed, the rolls of dough can stay in the refrigerator for several days before you slice and bake them.

1 cup unsalted butter, softened
1 cup brown sugar
1 tsp vanilla
2 egg yolks
1 tsp grated lemon rind (the zest, or colored part of the peel only)

1½ cups flour
1 cup yellow cornmeal
¼ tsp salt
2 tsp ground ginger

Beat the butter and sugar together in a large mixing bowl until well blended. Beat in the vanilla, egg yolks, and lemon rind.

In another bowl, stir and toss together the flour, cornmeal, salt, and ginger. Add to the butter-sugar mixture, and blend thoroughly until the dough is cohesive and completely mixed.

Divide the dough in half (it will be soft), and on a lightly floured surface, push, pat, and roll each piece into a cylinder about 7 inches long and 1½ inches in diameter. Wrap securely in plastic wrap (if you plan to refrigerate or freeze it) or waxed paper, and chill for a few hours, until firm

Preheat the oven to 350 degrees. With a thin sharp knife, cut the dough into rounds about ¼ inch thick. Place about an inch apart on buttered cookie sheets and bake for about 10 minutes. They should spread and puff just slightly, but should not brown. Remove from the sheets and cool on racks, then store in an an airtight container.

GINGERBREAD

Serves 12 to 16

A while ago, I attended a great gingerbread-tasting party in Berkeley. I wouldn't have missed it for anything. Oona Aven had made something like seventeen different recipes of gingerbread, and this is the one that was clearly the favorite. Oona is a great eater, a nurse, a runner, and, of course, an excellent baker.

If you've never used fresh ginger, this is a nice way to introduce yourself to it. It has much more pizzazz than the dried stuff. When you're grating ginger, use the finer part of the grater. Some ginger is stringy, and so it may be necessary to remove strings from the grated product.

Serve the gingerbread warm and plain, or with lemon curd (see page 231), or whipped cream. I happen to like plain best, but it tastes good no matter how you serve it.

½ cup unsalted butter, softened
½ cup dark brown sugar
¼ cup molasses
¼ cup dark Karo corn syrup
1 egg, beaten
¼ tsp salt

1½ cups flour
1 tsp baking soda
½ cup buttermilk, at room temperature
2-oz. knob of fresh ginger, peeled and grated

Cream together the butter and sugar. Add molasses, corn syrup, egg, and salt, and beat until smooth. Mix together the flour and baking soda. Whisk in half the flour/baking soda mixture, then half the buttermilk, and repeat. Stir in the ginger until it is well-dispersed.

Pour into an 8-inch square buttered pan, and bake at 350 degrees for 35 to 40 minutes. Serve warm or at room temperature with lemon curd (see page 231) or, perhaps, whipped cream.

FUDGY BROWNIES

*Makes 9 brownies,
more or less*

There are two schools of thought on brownies: fudgy and caky. Those of us who prefer fudgy are the real hard-core chocolate lovers. There are two *more* schools of thought with regard to nuts. The nut-lovers think they accentuate the chocolatiness, while the nut-haters begrudge the space the nuts take up. Well, these brownies are definitely fudgy, but whether or not nuts are included is up to you.

¾ cup brown sugar
⅓ cup unsalted butter
2 Tb water
1 cup (6 oz.) chocolate chips
1 tsp vanilla
1 tsp instant coffee

2 eggs, beaten
¾ cup flour
¼ tsp salt
¼ tsp baking soda
¾ cup walnuts, almonds or pecans, chopped and toasted (optional)

Combine sugar, butter, and water in a large saucepan. Bring just to a boil and remove from heat. Add chocolate chips, vanilla and coffee. Stir until chocolate melts. Beat in eggs. Sift together flour, salt, and baking soda. Add to chocolate mixture. Add nuts (if you wish). Pour into a greased 8-inch square pan, and bake at 325 degrees for 55 minutes. Should look slightly underbaked in the center.

PEPPERMINT PATTI'S BROWNIES

This variation on Fudgy Brownies is named for Patti Martin, who lives in Albion, just south of Mendocino. This is even more hard-core chocolate than the basic brownie recipe.

1 batch of Fudgy Brownies, cooled
¼ cup + 1½ Tb unsalted butter
½ lb. sifted powdered sugar

½ tsp peppermint extract
2 Tb heavy cream
3 oz. unsweetened chocolate

Melt ¼ cup butter in saucepan. Add sugar, peppermint extract, and heavy cream. Beat until creamy and smooth. Spread over cooled brownies, and refrigerate for 20 minutes.

Meanwhile, melt chocolate and 1½ tablespoons butter in top of a double boiler. Pour over the frosted brownies. Spread it around with a spatula.

AMAZON CHOCOLATE CAKE

Serves 12 to 16

I really don't know *why* we call it "Amazon"—but for some reason the name makes people laugh. We sell a tremendous amount of this in the restaurant. People will say, "Oh, Amazon Chocolate Cake. Ho ho ho. I'll have two pieces." Sometimes I wonder if we should give *all* our desserts funny names.

This cake is often pointed to as a curiosity, like a mayonnaise chocolate cake or a catsup chocolate cake, because it doesn't have any eggs or dairy products in it. Not only does it work, but it's actually an exemplary chocolate cake. It has what I think of as the "Duncan Hines crumb"—the one you see on the front of the cake mix boxes, that looks luscious and moist, with the fork poised over it. It's easy to make and tastes much more complex than it really is.

You can use the same batter as the basis for some wonderful cupcakes. That recipe comes next. Frost cake with Mocha Buttercream Frosting (see page 247).

3 cups flour	2 cups cold water
⅔ cup unsweetened cocoa	½ cup + 2 Tb corn oil
2 tsp baking soda	1 Tb vanilla
2 cups sugar	2 Tb white vinegar or strained lemon
1 tsp salt	juice

Mix together flour, cocoa, baking soda, sugar, and salt. Sift. In separate bowl, mix together water, corn oil, vanilla, and vinegar or lemon juice. Whisk together the wet and dry mixtures. Pour through strainer into a bowl, breaking up lumps and pressing them through. Mix again, and pour into 2 greased 9-inch round cake pans or one greased 9 × 13 × 2-inch pan. Tap the edge of the pan against the edge of the counter, or drop from 6 inches to floor several times to pop air bubbles. Bake at 350 degrees for 25 to 30 minutes.

AMAZON CREAM CHEESE CUPCAKES

The Amazon story has just been told (page 210). This recipe enhances the same batter and enables you to turn it into 3 dozen wonderful chocolate and cream cheese muffins.

Amazon Chocolate Cake batter (see page 210)
12 oz. natural cream cheese
2 eggs

½ cup sugar
1¼ cups chocolate chips
½ cup chopped walnuts

Combine cream cheese, eggs, sugar, chips, walnuts.

Fill 36 paper-lined muffin tins about ½ full of batter. Top with 1 generous tablespoon of cream cheese mixture. Bake at 350 degrees for 35 minutes.

CHOCOLATE SOUR CREAM FUDGE CAKE

Serves 12 to 16

This and the Amazon Chocolate Cake (page 210) are the two cakes in this book that could be photographed for the Duncan Hines cake mix box. Beautiful, moist, and luscious. This is actually a traditional American chocolate cake, with, dare I say, a few improvements, such as the Crème Fraîche Chocolate Frosting (see page 245). I always make it for birthdays, and for those adventuresome couples who want a chocolate wedding cake.

2 cups flour
2 t. baking soda
½ tsp salt
½ cup unsalted butter, softened
2¼ cups light or dark brown sugar
3 eggs

4 oz. bitter chocolate, melted and cooled
1½ tsp pure vanilla
1 cup sour cream
1 cup very strong hot liquid coffee

Sift together flour, baking soda and salt. Beat butter, sugar and eggs for 5 minutes in the bowl of an electric mixer, until very light and fluffy. Beat in chocolate and vanilla. Stir in about ⅓ of the dry ingredients, half the sour cream, another ⅓ of dry ingredients, the rest of the sour cream, and finally the remainder of the dry ingredients. Stir *just* until mixed.

Stir in hot coffee, and pour into 2 9-inch square pans greased and lined with waxed paper. Strike each pan on the edge of the counter or drop several times onto the floor from a height of 6 inches to release air bubbles. Bake at 350 degrees for 35 minutes. Cool pans on a wire rack for 15 minutes. Run a knife around the edge, turn out, and cool completely.

The suggested frosting is described on page 245.

MOM'S BANANA CAKE

A little violin music please. This is another one of my mom's recipes. My mom is famous for making very simple, homey desserts. Her cobblers are the only ones I've ever been able to eat. Everybody else's are like lead; hers are light. This banana cake that tastes elegant all by itself—and even more so with a little embellishment I made it one day for a friend's birthday and filled it with rum crème pâtissière. (Rum and bananas are a common combination in gourmet banana circles.)

The cake is made with oil; it's a complete disaster with butter. I've even made it with chocolate crème pâtissière—but then I've tried almost everything in my repertoire with chocolate.

2 cups flour	2 eggs
1 tsp baking soda	1½ cups sugar
1 tsp baking powder	½ cup chopped, lightly toasted walnuts (see Boozie's Apple Cake page 219)
1 tsp salt	
½ cup corn oil	Crème Pâtissière (see page 246)— plain, chocolate, or rum-flavored
½ cup buttermilk	
1¼ cups mashed ripe bananas	

Step 1: Make batter

Sift together flour, baking soda, baking powder, and salt. Place in the large bowl of an electric mixer. Add corn oil, buttermilk, and bananas. Beat to form a smooth batter—about 30 seconds.

Step 2: Make egg-sugar mixture

In a separate bowl, beat 2 eggs until thick and foamy. Gradually add sugar, and continue beating for 3 minutes. Add walnuts.

Step 3: Blend and cook

Fold egg-sugar mixture into batter. Pour into 2 waxed-paper-lined 9-inch round pans. Whack on edge of counter, or drop 6 inches to floor several times to release air bubbles. Bake at 350 degrees for 30 to 35 minutes. Let sit on rack for 10 minutes, then run a knife around the cakes, and turn them out. When cool, fill with rum crème pâtissière.

Alternatively, you can split both cake layers horizontally, make a 4-layer cake with 3 levels of crème pâtissière filling.

POPPY SEED POUND CAKE

I love poppy seeds in bread, and they're great in this cake, too. Cakes like this were really the rage for a while. I saw recipes everywhere, but none was exactly what I had in mind, so I made one to my liking. Usually I'm averse to cakes that have a syrup or sugar sauce poured on top because they are often too sweet and goopy, but for some reason, this one doesn't come out like that.

In the restaurant, we serve this by the slice for breakfast or lunch. You can warm it if you like.

CAKE
1½ cups unsalted butter, softened
2 cups white sugar
6 eggs, beaten
3 Tb finely grated lemon rind
1 Tb finely grated orange rind
1 tsp pure vanilla extract
¾ cup poppy seeds

2 cups + 2 Tb sifted white flour
2 tsp baking powder
¾ tsp salt
¾ cup + 2 Tb milk

SYRUP
2 Tb orange juice, strained
¼ cup lemon juice, strained
¼ cup sugar

In the bowl of an electric mixer, cream together butter and 2 cups of sugar until very light and fluffy (about 2 minutes). Add eggs, both rinds, vanilla, and poppy seeds, and beat for 2 minutes. Sift together flour, baking powder, and salt, and add to poppy mixture in 3 parts, alternating with the milk.

Pour into a greased and floured 10-inch tube pan. Bake at 350 degrees for 60 minutes. Let cool on wire rack for 10 minutes. Pull center insert out. Do not remove cake from tube.

Combine the strained juices and ¼ cup sugar, and stir to dissolve. Spoon over cake evenly. The cake will keep for 3 days.

APPLE OATMEAL CRISP

Serves 8

One of Mendocino county's main legal crops is apples, and we see a lot of them, year 'round. I like homey desserts, and apple crisp epitomizes that for me. I've elaborated on the standard one by adding more spices than is customary. It's really satisfying, especially when topped with vanilla custard sauce or vanilla ice cream.

It's a good dish to make with children. Just peel and slice the apples, mix the liquid, throw on the other stuff, and it's practically done.

If you can't get locally grown apples, then use Pippin, Gravenstein, or Granny Smiths.

6 firm apples, peeled, cored, and cut in ¼-inch slices
juice of 1 lemon, strained
rind of 1 lemon, grated
¼ cup water, apple juice, brandy, or Calvados
¾ cup light brown sugar
½ cup unsalted butter

¾ cup flour
½ cup regular oats
1 tsp cinnamon
½ tsp ginger
¼ tsp nutmeg
optional toppings: vanilla ice cream, whipped cream, or Vanilla Custard Sauce (see page 248)

Mix together apples, lemon juice, lemon rind, and water, apple juice, brandy or Calvados. Place in a buttered 9-inch round cake pan.

Using an electric mixer at slow speed, blend sugar, butter, flour, oats, cinnamon, ginger, and nutmeg, until crumbly. Scatter evenly on top of apples. Bake at 350 degrees for 1 hour. Serve warm with one of the optional toppings if desired.

CRÈME FRAÎCHE CUSTARD TART

I invented this recipe. It's quite elegant, and on the delicate side—basically a flaky pre-baked tart dough crust that's filled with a crème fraîche cream cheese custard baked ever-so-briefly, then filled with fruit. What I like about it is that it's not too sweet, and it's got a lot of very good flavors and textures in it. I've made it with raspberries, huckleberries, and blueberries, and I've baked it with sautéed apples in it. Both variations follow the basic recipe.

3 oz. natural cream cheese	2 egg yolks
½ cup Crème Fraîche (see page 244)	fruit topping of your choice
	Tart Dough Shell (see page 230)

Beat cream cheese until smooth. Add crème fraîche and egg yolks, and beat until smooth. Pour into tart shell and bake at 375 degrees for 5 to 8 minutes, just until it is barely set. It should *not* be firm, but rather quivery.

Cool on a wire rack for 30 minutes, then cover with fruit topping.

TART WITH SAUTÉED APPLES

1 peeled Granny Smith apple, thinly sliced	juice of ½ lemon
2 Tb unsalted butter	pinch nutmeg
rind of ½ lemon	2 pinches cinnamon
	1 Tb brown sugar

Sauté apple slices in butter for 10 minutes, stirring frequently. Cover and cook for 2 more minutes. Watch closely. Add lemon juice and rind, nutmeg, cinnamon, and brown sugar. Cook 1 minute, until the liquid is just absorbed and apples are edible without further cooking.

Strew apples over bottom of tart, pour in custard, dust with additional cinnamon, and bake for 10 minutes at 375 degrees until just barely set. Remove and let cool.

HUCKLEBERRY, BLUEBERRY, OR RASPBERRY TOPPING

3 cups berries
3 Tb cassis or raspberry syrup
   (Vedrenne is a good brand) or kirsch
1 Tb sugar

Place 2 cups of berries on the tart in concentric circles, starting from the outside. Place them closely together, so that as little white as possible shows.

Make the glaze by placing 1 cup of berries, the cassis, syrup or kirsch and sugar in a heavy saucepan. Cook over medium heat, stirring to dissolve sugar, and to mash the berries. When slightly thickened, strain. Press as much as possible through a strainer.

With a small pastry brush, carefully paint the glaze onto the berries. Delicacy is important for the appearance, so this will be painstaking.

Serve the tart within 3 hours.

MOM'S BAKED APPLES

(The following introduction comes from Mom, herself, Anne Fox. My mom has some definite opinions about apples.)

"For all their hominess and apparent good will, apples are more mysterious and deceptive than we have been led to believe. They vary greatly in texture, flavor and baking time. Although I like McIntosh and Rome Beauty best for baking, other cooks have their own favorites. Apples lend themselves to many fillings and basting liquids. The following is a general rule-of-thumb recipe, which can easily be modified."

4 8-oz. (approx.) apples: McIntosh or Rome Beauty

juice from ½ lemon, strained

¼ cup chopped dried fruit (any kind or kinds)

¼ cup brown sugar, firmly packed

¼ cup chopped nuts and/or coconut

½ cup dry vermouth, or red or white wine

¾ cup water

¼ cup brown sugar or honey

½ tsp cinnamon

⅔ cup heavy cream

Core apples, leaving bottoms intact, creating a hollow space that can hold about 2 tablespoonsful of filling. Peel the top inch of each apple. Place in an 8 × 8-inch baking dish. Sprinkle lemon juice over apples, and into dish.

Mix together the fruit, ¼ cup brown sugar, and nuts and/or coconut. Fill cavities with this mixture, tamping down with the handle of a wooden spoon.

Make basting liquid by mixing together the vermouth or wine, water, and ¼ cup brown sugar or honey, and pour into pan.

Sprinkle apples with cinnamon and bake uncovered at 400 degrees, basting every 15 minutes until they are tender, soft, and slightly split. This can take anywhere from 45 to 85 minutes, and all the apples in the pan may not be ready at the same time.

Remove to individual dishes as the apples are finished cooking. Baste evenly with the remaining syrupy juices.

Serve slightly warm with heavy cream.

BOOZIE'S APPLE CAKE

Serves 12

This recipe comes from Marcia Sloane. There's no booze in it; Boozie is a real human being (Cata Bingham's godmother). For us, one good thing about this cake is that it provides a great way to use up the large number of apples that we are always being given by local orchard-owners. It's a nice, spicy coffee cake dessert. Easy as apple cake to make. You don't even have to pare the apples. If it seems too simple for a "company" dessert, well, vanilla ice cream never hurt anything, did it?

I advocate the toasting of walnuts, simply because it enhances the flavor. If you liked walnuts before, you'll really love them toasted. Instructions below.

4 cups apples, unpeeled, cored and
    cut into ½-inch cubes
2 cups flour
2 tsp baking soda
¾ tsp salt
2 tsp cinnamon
2 eggs, beaten
¼ cup white sugar
2 cups brown sugar + ¼ cup water
1 tsp pure vanilla extract
½ cup corn oil
1 cup coarsely chopped walnuts

Bake walnut meats at 325 degrees for 10 to 15 minutes. Check them by eating one, and seeing if it tastes toasty. To remove the brown skin, put baked meats in a sieve or strainer and agitate them. The brown stuff starts falling off. Alternatively, you can rub them in a towel.

Sift together flour, baking soda, salt, and cinnamon, and set aside. Beat eggs, white sugar, brown sugar + water, vanilla and corn oil, then add flour mixture and toasted nuts. When thoroughly blended, add apples, and stir.

Pour into a greased 9 × 13 × 2-inch pan and bake at 325 degrees for 65 to 75 minutes. The cake will appear moist but not wet.

CARROT (OR APPLE) CAKE

Ordinarily, I would never consider eating carrot cake, much less including one in this book. The only reason I did this one was because my friends, Kate O'Shea and Michael Gabel once insisted on a carrot cake for their wedding. So I fiddled around, and came up with something that was as "sophisticated" as it could be, considering what it was.

Usually those ubiquitous carrot cakes you see on everyone's menus are much too sweet. This one really is self-respecting. Too bad the whole world jumped on the bandwagon. And if you are feeling snobbish about carrot cakes, as I have been, you can make this with apples instead.

Most people seem to want cream cheese frosting on this, but it works fine if you just sprinkle on a little powdered sugar and call it a tea cake.

¾ cup corn oil
1 cup brown sugar
⅔ cup white sugar
4 eggs
1 cup white flour
¾ cup + 2 Tb whole wheat flour
1 tsp salt
2 tsp baking soda
2 tsp baking powder
1 Tb cinnamon

½ tsp nutmeg
1 tsp ground ginger
3 cups finely shredded carrots or grated apples
1 8½-oz. can crushed, drained pineapple
⅔ cup chopped toasted walnuts (see Boozie's Apple Cake page 219)
2 tsp powdered sugar

Place oil, brown and white sugars, and eggs in bowl of an electric mixer, and blend. In another bowl, sift togehter both flours, salt, baking soda, baking powder, cinnamon, nutmeg, and ginger. Add flour mixture slowly to oil mixture. Add carrots (or apples), pineapple, and nuts. Pour into greased, floured 9 × 13-inch pan.

Bake at 325 for 55 minutes. Let cool, then sift powdered sugar on top before serving.

HAZELNUT TORTE

This is technically a torte, which means the main ingredients are just nuts, eggs, and sugar—no flour. I like it because I love the flavor of hazelnuts. It can be made very quickly. The only special skill needed is the ability to fold things in. It's simple, yet elegant: a traditional European dessert.

It's also quite flexible. You can use apricot or other fruit jam. Hazelnuts and chocolate go well together, too. You can put chocolate in the center, chocolate on the outside, chocolate in both places.

When you turn this out, it doesn't look beautiful, but that's quite all right, because (a)it tastes awfully good, and (b)you're going to cover it with whipped cream anyway.

8 egg whites
pinch salt
1 cup sugar
8 egg yolks
1 tsp vanilla
2⅔ cups ground hazelnuts

4 Tb brandy
½ cup (after straining) apricot or raspberry jam, heated and strained
1 cup heavy cream
2 Tb powdered sugar

Beat egg whites with salt until they hold soft peaks. Add 1 cup of the sugar 1 tablespoon at a time, continuing to beat about 15 seconds after each addition, and then for 5 more minutes. Mixture will be very stiff.

Beat yolks with vanilla for 2 minutes. Fold whites into yolks partially, then sprinkle hazelnuts on top. Fold together, and divide between 2 9-inch round pans, greased and lined with waxed paper, then greased again. Bake 45 minutes at 350 degrees. Remove from oven and let cool on wire racks for 20 minutes *before* turning out of pans. Trim the outer edges so that they are even with the sunken middles.

Sprinkle each layer with 2 tablespoons of brandy, and sandwich them together with jam. With a long metal spatula, spread remaining jam thinly over the top and sides of torte.

Let set for 1 hour in the refrigerator.

Whip chilled cream and 2 tablespoons of powdered sugar just until stiff peaks are formed. Spread lavishly over top and sides, saving some for decorating the top and sides with rosettes, using a pastry bag and a star top. Or, alternatively frost with Chocolate Crème Fraîche Frosting (see page 245).

Refrigerate until ½ hour before serving.

CHOCOLATE MARZIPAN TORTE

This is a dessert I developed for some friends who live for marzipan. Yes, I am aware of the distinction between almond paste and marzipan—how the one evolves into the other—so save your informative letters. I simply don't like the name "Chocolate Almond Paste Torte." The almond paste in question was developed by Rosemary Manell, artist, friend, cook, and food stylist.

The recipe takes a lot of space to describe, but it isn't that complex; it simply has to be done just right. Be especially careful not to process the almonds for too long. They grow oily and turn into nut butter, and the process is irreversible.

The quantities are given in volume for convenience, and also in weight for precision. (Most professional bakers go by weight rather than volume.)

ALMOND PASTE

3 oz. almonds, blanched
¼ cup sugar
½ tsp lemon juice
1½ Tb water
½ tsp almond extract

2 Tb + 1 tsp warm liquid coffee
½ cup unsalted butter
½ cup sugar
3 large eggs, separated
pinch of salt

TORTE

½ cup (2 oz.) almond paste (see above)
4 oz. semisweet chocolate
1 cup (4 oz.) ground almonds

GLAZE

6 oz. semisweet chocolate
6 Tb heavy cream, warmed
1 tsp dry instant coffee

Step 1: Make almond paste

Make almond paste by grinding almonds in a food processor with a steel S-blade until coarse. Add sugar and grind until very fine. With machine running, add lemon juice, water, and almond extract, and run for 15 seconds. The mixture will be soft and crumbly. Store excess in the refrigerator.

Step 2: Make torte

Preheat oven to 350 degrees, arranging a rack in the middle of the oven. Liberally butter an 8-inch springform pan and line with waxed paper. Butter again.

Slowly melt the chocolate in a double boiler. Add ½ cup almond paste, and stir to blend. (The mixture will have a nubbly consistency.)

Add coffee, stir to combine, remove from heat, and let cool.

Beat butter and sugar until fluffy, add egg yolks one at a time, while beating, and add ground almonds while beating at slow speed. Add cooled chocolate mixture, and beat until combined.

Scrape the mixture into a bowl. Add salt to egg whites, and beat until stiff but not dry. Stir ¼ of the egg whites into the chocolate mixture, then gently fold in the remaining whites.

Pour batter into the buttered pan. Bake at 350 degrees for 35 to 45 minutes. The torte will still be slightly "wet" in the center, and it will deflate slightly when removed from oven. Cool on a rack for 20 minutes, release spring, and let cake sit 10 minutes more. Place a plate upside down over the cake and invert. Gently remove bottom of pan, sliding a knife between pan bottom and cake for easy removal. Peel waxed paper off slowly.

Step 3: Make glaze

Melt chocolate slowly in top of double boiler. Add cream and coffee, and whisk together until smooth. Remove from heat and let sit 10 to 15 minutes with the whisk still in the mixture, then stir again. Glaze will be slightly thickened, but not as thick as traditional frostings. Use it immediately. Pour glaze over the thoroughly cooled cake, helping to cover the sides evenly by using a spatula.

LINZERTORTE

I like this traditional German recipe because it's ultra-spicy. In fact, it's really a tart, not a torte. It doesn't have a dense crust like a pie; it's more like a soft cookie. The cocoa comes through as a mysterious flavor. Traditionally it is made with raspberry or apricot jam.

The classic recipe calls for a lattice top, requiring laborious interweaving of strips of dough, which makes a mess, since the dough is quite rich. One day, inspiration struck. I put the dough into a pastry tube, and squished out a fake lattice top. Lo and behold, it came out looking just as good as the real thing.

This gets better with age. It is even better on the third day, as happens to many spicy things. Complete hedonists may wish to add whipped cream before serving.

½ cup butter, softened
⅔ cup sugar
1 tsp lemon rind, finely grated
¼ tsp salt
1 egg
¾ cup + 2 Tb white flour

⅔ cup finely ground almonds
½ tsp cinnamon
¼ tsp cloves
1 Tb cocoa
1 cup raspberry or apricot jam
whipped cream (optional)

Beat butter, sugar, lemon rind and salt together until fluffy, about 3 minutes. Add the rest of the ingredients (except for the jam and whipped cream) to combine. Refrigerate for 1 hour. Reserve ⅓ of dough for lattice crust.

Press dough into a 9-inch springform pan. Fill with jam. Using a pastry tube filled with the reserved dough, make a lattice top: five strips in each direction. Refrigerate for ½ hour, then bake at 325 degrees for 50 minutes. The crust will be slightly soft. Let cool. Remove from pan. Garnish with whipped cream, if you wish, just before serving.

PECAN TARTS

Chris Hock has been the bookkeeper for Cafe Beaujolais for years. She has stuck with us through the bad times and the good. When she saw this book being put together, she revealed to me that she had a pecan tart recipe that had been in her family for many years. So we tried them. They were fabulous. We made 24 and they were devoured in minutes. They're very rich and wonderful little things that are great for tea.

You could use other nuts, but pecans are rich and sweet, as nuts go, and just right for this. You can use larger muffin tins, but some people may be hard pressed to finish a larger tart.

1 cup flour	¾ cup light brown sugar, packed
½ cup natural cream cheese	1 Tb butter, melted
½ cup unsalted butter, softened	¾ cup coarsely chopped pecans
⅛ tsp salt	pinch salt
1 egg white	1 tsp vanilla

Preheat oven to 400 degrees. Mix together flour, cream cheese, ½ cup butter, and salt, using an electric mixer or a food processor fitted with a steel S-blade, until a dough forms. Shape dough into 24 balls. Refrigerate 30 minutes.

Meanwhile, make filling by beating egg white with a fork until light and very foamy. Add sugar, 1 tablespoon melted butter, pecans, salt, and vanilla, and mix in a large bowl until combined.

Press balls into teacake tins (muffin tins which are 1¼ inch in diameter across the bottom) up to the rim to form the shells. Fill each shell with ¾ teaspoon filling. Bake 15 minutes at 400 degrees, and then 10 minutes at 250 degrees. Cool in tins before removing. They will come out easily.

NUT TART

This is your basic generic nut tart. My mom made something like it years ago, and I liked it a lot. Then we fiddled around with it in the restaurant to make it just a little better. I like to cook the crust frozen; there's less shrinkage, and it just comes out better.

I love this dessert. It's such a deceptively simple-appearing dish, but it tastes so good. One thing that's really nice is that you can freeze it at different stages. You can make the dough and freeze it. You can put the dough in pans and *then* freeze it.

One caution: be sure to let the tart stay in the oven long enough. Some people see it bubbling, and they assume it must be done, but that's not true. It must stay in until it is richly brown. That extra time pays off. It will taste fantastic. If you want to gild the lily, add some vanilla ice cream.

DOUGH	FILLING
1⅓ cup white flour	½ cup sugar
⅛ tsp salt	pinch salt
⅔ cup unsalted butter	2 Tb orange liqueur or kirsch
4 tsp sugar	¾ cup heavy cream
1 tsp vanilla	1 cup sliced almonds, chopped walnuts, chopped pecans, or lightly toasted chopped macadamia nuts
1 Tb water	

Step 1. *Make tart shell*

Mix all dough ingredients until well-blended. The dough will ball up. (It is not harmed by extra handling, as is flaky pie crust.) Press dough evenly into a 9-inch removable-bottom quiche pan. It should be just under ¼ inch thick on the bottom. Leave about ¼ inch above the pan rim to allow for inevitable shrinkage. Place in a plastic bag in the freezer for at least 30 minutes, (or up to several weeks).

Preheat oven to 400 degrees and place pan with frozen dough in oven. Bake for 30 minutes, until golden brown. Remove from oven and let cool completely (at least ½ hour) on a rack.

Step 2: *Make filling*

Combine all filling ingredients and let sit 30 minutes. Stir, and pour into baked, cooled tart shell. Place a piece of aluminum foil directly under the tart tin to catch the drips. Bake at 400 degrees for 45 to 50 minutes (50 minutes with macadamia nuts), until carmelized and richly brown.

MOCHA FUDGE ALMOND PIE

This is a killer dessert. It is *so* rich, I can't even lick my fingers after making it. How rich is this dessert? This dessert is so rich that we actually use whipped cream to cut the richness! The flavor is just incredible. It doesn't seem like enough for 10 people, but I assure you it is. Well, some people might cut it into 8 pieces, but you'd better do that under medical supervision.

1¼ cup graham cracker crumbs
6 Tb unsalted butter, melted
2 cups heavy cream
1 oz. bitter chocolate
5 oz. semisweet chocolate
1 Tb instant coffee (powder or granules)

5 egg yolks
1 cup blanched almonds, coarsely chopped and toasted almonds (chop first, then toast)
2 Tb powdered sugar

Step 1: Make graham cracker crust

Stir together graham cracker crumbs and melted butter. Press into a 9-inch pie pan. The crust should be the same thickness on the sides and bottom—about ⅛ inch to ³⁄₁₆ inch thick. Bake at 375 degrees for 7 minutes. Remove from oven and cool on a rack.

Step 2: Make mocha mix

In a heavy saucepan, place 1 cup of the heavy cream, both chocolates, and instant coffee. Stir over low heat until dissolved. Remove and let cool for 5 minutes.

Step 3: Assemble pie

Beat the egg yolks with an electric mixer, and gradually add the chocolate mixture to them, until thoroughly blended and very creamy. Stir in the almonds, and pour into the cooled graham cracker crust. Chill for at least 5 hours.

Step 4: Make whipped cream and serve

Whip together the remaining heavy cream and powdered sugar. Top pie with whipped cream and serve.

ANNI'S FUDGE PIE

Serves 8

I was given this recipe in strictest secrecy by Anni Amberger, who used to bake at Cruchon's Restaurant in Berkeley. But that was long ago, and now Anni says it's all right to tell the world.

My own way of eating has changed radically since those days. I used to think fudge pie was heaven on earth, but I just can't eat this much chocolate any more.

This is a no-nonsense dessert. You make the crust—an unbaked pie shell, whip together the chocolate stuff, and bake it. And that's it. You can freeze it. You can even eat it frozen if you can't wait.

It's made with bitter chocolate, so it's very chocolatey. It's not adulterated with a single nut. It's hard core chocolate that sets your heart pumping. We serve it with whipped cream and a sprinkling of cocoa on the top. Très chic.

4 oz. unsalted butter
4 oz. unsweetened chocolate,
  melted and cooled
¾ cup sugar
3 eggs, beaten

1 tsp vanilla
1 cup heavy cream
2 Tb sugar
pie shell (see page 229)

Bake the pie shell "blind" (empty), with foil and beans or ceramic "marbles" made for the purpose, to weigh it down. After 20 minutes, remove the foil and weights, and bake 5 more minutes. Cool for at least 30 minutes before using.

Melt the butter and chocolate together, and cool. Beat together sugar, eggs, and vanilla. Add the chocolate and butter, stir to blend and pour into the pie shell. Bake at 375 degrees for 30 minutes on the bottom rack. (The top will crack, but it's OK.) Cool and serve at room temperature, with whipped cream and some cocoa sprinkled on top.

STANDARD PIE CRUST

8 Tb unsalted butter
4 Tb lard
1¾ cup flour

½ tsp salt
about ⅓ cup ice water

Cut butter and lard into very small pieces and place in freezer for at least 15 minutes. Place flour and salt in the bowl of a food processor fitted with a steel S-blade and process for a few seconds to blend. Add butter and lard pieces, and process until they are cut into the flour, about 3 seconds. Immediately add ice water and blend for about 3 more seconds. Dough should form on blade. DO NOT OVERMIX. Turn out and quickly press into a round about 1 inch thick. Wrap in plastic wrap and a plastic bag, and place in refrigerator for at least 2½ hours. (Dough can be kept in the refrigerator up to 2 days, or frozen for longer storage.)

Roll dough out on a lightly floured board with a lightly floured rolling pin until it is about ³⁄₁₆ inches thick and very even. Place in a 9-inch pie pan, gently pressing the dough into the pan where necessary. Finish the rim of the dough in your favorite fashion, trimming off excess. Prick bottom with fork. Put shell as is in freezer for 30 minutes to use it right away. Otherwise, carefully set in a plastic bag, close tightly, and freeze.

To use, either bake according to the specific instructions for your chosen filling or bake "blind" (empty) by placing a sheet of buttered foil on the crust to cover completely, and weighing it down with beans or ceramic "marbles" made for this purpose. Bake at 425 degrees for up to 25 minutes, depending on the type of pie you are making.

TART DOUGH

Makes two 9-inch
tart crusts

This is a particularly good recipe because you don't have to worry about overhandling it the way you do with pie dough. The dough is very short— a high proportion of butter to flour—so you get what some people call a cookie crust, but it's lighter than most cookies. It's a good foil for fresh fruit or for heavier fillings, like lemon curd, that need to be offset.

The dough has to be pressed into the pan. The notion of a press-in pie dough is unusual for many people; they fiddle around rolling it out and being careful with it, but you don't have to with this.

2 cups white flour
3 Tb sugar
2 pinches salt

1 cup unsalted butter, cold, and cut in 8 pieces
grated rind of 1 lemon

Mix together flour, sugar, and salt in the large bowl of an electric mixer or the bowl of a food processor fitted with a steel S-blade. Add butter and lemon rind and mix until dough forms. Press into 2 9-inch removable-bottom tart pans or 8 4-inch removable bottom tart pans. Bake at 375 degrees for 15 to 18 minutes, until golden brown. This dough must be prebaked and cooled totally before it is filled.

LEMON CURD

This is a very rich lemon custard with very few ingredients. We make it at the restaurant in huge quantities but still can't keep enough of it in stock. Our recipe calls for 80 egg yolks, plus 50 whole eggs. We serve it as a parfait with whipped cream, or in a tiny tart (see page for a good tart dough). It keeps for 3 weeks, and you can freeze it, although I can't imagine why, since it disappears so fast.

It tastes very fresh, very tart. When people go out to eat, they often want to justify to themselves that they're really not overeating, and for some reason, they equate lemons (and apples) with something healthy. They say, "Oh that sounds nice and light." Ah, well.

grated peel from 5 lemons
1 cup + 2 Tb lemon juice (5 to 7 lemons' worth)
1½ cup white sugar
½ tsp salt

6 whole eggs
12 egg yolks
1 cup + 2 Tb unsalted butter, cut into small pieces

Place peel, juice, sugar, salt, eggs, and yolks in the top of a double boiler. Mix with a whisk over medium heat. Do not let water touch the bottom of the top pot, and do not let the water boil, or you'll have scrambled curd.

Whisk continuously for 15 minutes until thick. Add butter, piece by piece, and whisk in thoroughly. Strain this mixture and store in the refrigerator for up to 3 weeks. Can also be frozen.

FANTASIA PARFAIT

We use our espresso machine to make a drink called a Cafe Fantasia: espresso, almond-flavored syrup, and chocolate. It's a very popular drink. There are people who have had three at one sitting, then flown away. So we decided it would be fun to make a dessert based on those three flavors. It's very creamy and satisfying.

My mother looked at this recipe and said, "Serves 10? Are you kidding? It'll serve *16*." Well it all depends on the size of the glass—and your capacity for rich desserts.

6 egg yolks	½ cup Amaretto di Saronno
⅓ cup water	1½ tsp almond extract
⅔ cup sugar	2 cups heavy cream
8 oz. unsweetened chocolate	grated chocolate for garnish
3 Tb liquid espresso or very strong coffee	

Beat the egg yolks in a large bowl of an electric mixer until thick and light colored.

In a saucepan, cook sugar and water on moderate heat until the sugar is dissolved. Raise heat and boil while stirring until the temperature reads 220 degrees on a candy thermometer.

Remove bowl with beaten yolks from electric mixer. Being very careful not to get burned with the hot syrup, pour the syrup in a thin stream into the beaten eggs, while whisking by hand constantly. Continue to whisk until cool (about 5 minutes).

Stir espresso, chocolate, amaretto, and almond extract in a saucepan over gentle heat, just until the chocolate is melted. Stir into the yolk mixture until thoroughly blended.

In another bowl, beat whipping cream until it forms soft peaks and fold into chocolate mixture. Divide evenly into parfait glasses, and freeze for at least 3 hours. Garnish with grated chocolate.

VERY RICH VANILLA OR ESPRESSO ICE CREAM

Makes about 8 cups

In making these ice creams, I do something that I've never seen anyone else do. I heat the half and half and heavy cream, let it cool, and toss it all, *including the bean*, into the blender. This results in an extremely strong vanilla flavor. In the restaurant, we serve this with little French fan wafer cookies called *gaufrettes*, or sometimes with delicious almond butter cookies Jeffery Garcia makes for us. If the mixture curdles, let it cool for 20 minutes and blend it briefly. It actually uncurdles very nicely.

2 cups half and half
3 cups heavy cream
½ vanilla bean, split down center
16 egg yolks
1⅓ cup sugar

FOR VANILLA ICE CREAM
2 tsp pure vanilla extract

FOR EXPRESSO ICE CREAM
6 Tb ground espresso
⅔ cup liquid espresso

Bring half and half, heavy cream, and vanilla bean to a boil in a heavy saucepan. Let cool, then whirl in a blender for 10 seconds to draw more flavor from the bean. Strain, and discard bean after scraping whatever remains into the cream. Discard the raggle-taggle bean shreds.

Cream yolks and sugar together with an electric beater until thick and lighter colored. Add cream. Whisk together, and pour back into saucepan. Over medium heat, bring to 180 degrees stirring constantly. Remove from heat and immediately strain into a bowl. Place this bowl into a larger bowl filled with ice.

For espresso ice cream, add both coffees. For vanilla, add vanilla extract. Chill mixture thoroughly, place in an ice cream maker, and churn according to manufacturer's directions.

Transfer to a container with a tight-fitting top and freeze. Best when served within 24 hours.

LEMON ICE CREAM

When we serve this in the restaurant, people usually say, "Oh it's so nice to have something light after dinner." I think they're fooled by the tart taste of the lemon because this dessert is actually not light. People equate citrus with light and healthy. Well, maybe if you drink pure lemon juice.

5 Tb lemon juice, strained	1 pinch salt
grated rind of 2 lemons	⅛ tsp nutmeg
¾ cup white sugar	more nutmeg, toasted walnuts,
2 cups heavy cream	mints (optional)

Stir together all ingredients, making sure sugar is dissolved. Pour into an 8-inch square pan and place in your freezer. (You can also strain it before freezing, if you'd prefer a perfectly smooth texture.)

Every 30 minutes, stir, taking care to scrape the outside frozen parts into the middle. It will be ready in about 3 hours.

Optionally, top with nutmeg or toasted walnuts, and serve with a sprig of mint.

CARAMEL LACE ICE CREAM DESSERT

In addition to her amazing caramels (see page 205), Barbara Holzrichter uses the same terrific ingredients and care to produce a line of dessert sauces. She created this recipe as an excuse to have something pleasant to put underneath the sauce, because there's a limit to how much you can eat by dipping your finger in the jar without feeling excessively guilty. So you make these buttery cookies, fill them with ice cream, and top them with one of the irresistible Grand Finale sauces (which may be acquired through the mail; see page 256).

¾ cup finely chopped almonds
½ cup unsalted butter, cut into tablespoon-sized pieces
½ cup sugar
1 Tb flour

2 Tb heavy cream
ice cream (any flavor)
Grand Finale Sauce (any flavor— I love the mocha sauce more than I should.)

In a heavy saucepan, combine all ingredients except ice cream and sauce. Cook over low heat, stirring constantly until the butter melts. Drop by teaspoonsful 3 inches apart on greased and floured 10 × 15-inch baking sheet. (Be sure to bang the pan upside down to remove excess flour.) Do not crowd the cookies. Bake at 350 degrees for about 8 minutes, or until light brown and still bubbling in the center.

Cool only until the edge of the cookie is firm enough to lift with a metal spatula. Transfer to a rack and cool completely. Makes about 36.

To assemble, place a scoop of ice cream on a serving dish. Place 1 wafer on each side of scoop, like ear muffs. Pour sauce over ice cream.

CHOCOLATE TOASTED-NUT ICE CREAM

This is hard-core. One of the richest desserts we have. In the restaurant, I'm tempted to demand people's ID's before I agree to serve this to them. It's really intense. The coffee brings out the chocolate flavor. I prefer to make it with almonds, but many people like hazelnuts better. If you use them, pay attention to the instruction for removing the skin, or you'll have flaky nut skin in your mouth. As with all ice creams containing egg yolks, this works especially well with a home ice cream-making machine.

12 oz. semisweet chocolate
2 oz. unsweetened chocolate
1 Tb instant coffee
6 Tb liquid coffee
1⅓ cups half and half
1⅓ cups heavy cream

8 egg yolks
¾ cup + 2 Tb sugar
1⅓ cup almonds, hazelnuts or pecans, toasted and coarsely chopped

Step 1: Toast nuts

For walnuts, bake nut meats at 325 degrees for 10 to 15 minutes. Agitate in sieve or strainer or rub with towel to remove brown skin. For hazelnuts, bake for 15 to 20 minutes at 350 degrees. Remove brown skin by rolling nuts around in a dish towel—a laborious, boring, and very important task. For pecans, toast, and use as is.

Step 2: Prepare other components

In the top of a double boiler, melt both chocolates together with both coffees. Set aside.

In a separate saucepan, scald the half and half and heavy cream, and set aside.

In the large bowl of an electric mixer, beat the egg yolks and sugar until thick and lemon-colored (about 2 minutes). Slowly pour in hot cream and beat with a whisk. Place back on heat and beat constantly until the mixture reaches 180 degrees. Remove immediately and pour through a strainer into a large bowl.

Add chocolate mixture, stir, and place bowl into a larger bowl filled with ice. Stir occasionally until cold. Add the nuts. Pour into an ice cream maker.

Step 3: Make ice cream

Make the ice cream following the specific instructions for your ice cream machine. Transfer finished ice cream to a container with a tightly fitting top, and freeze for at least 3 hours before serving.

FRESH STRAWBERRY SORBET

Serves 4 to 6

Sorbet (pronounced soar-bay) is an ice. What impresses me about this recipe is that it comes out tasting very strongly of strawberries, even if the berries aren't that great to begin with. It's extremely simple to make. You can actually use almost any kind of berries—blue, black, boysen, rasp, whatever—but if you are using berries with seeds, strain the puréed berries before measuring them. We have fresh mint growing outside our door, so we serve sorbet with a mint garnish. It's a nice dessert when you want something frozen, but you don't want ice cream. It's a treat, and lower in calories than many desserts, so you don't have to feel guilty about it.

I have an aversion to cooked strawberries. They turn grey and look unappetizing. So this is a great thing to do with leftovers of less-than-wonderful berries.

⅔ to 1 cup sugar (depending on sweetness of berries)
1 cup water

2 cups fresh strawberry purée
juice from ½ lemon, strained
juice from ½ orange, strained

In a saucepan, combined sugar and water. Bring to a boil, stirring occasionally, and boil for 6 minutes. Let cool slightly, and stir in purée and juices.

Pour mixture into an 8-inch square pan and freeze until mushy. Stir with a fork, to break up ice crystals, every 30 minutes for about 3½ hours. Serve with mint garnish. Best served within 24 hours.

CREAMY CHEESECAKE

Serves 10 to 12

My mom said, "Oh, why are you including that? *Everybody* has a cake with cream cheese." But I swear, I've never eaten one this good. The reason is that it's not as sweet as most other cheesecakes, and it's very, very creamy. A lot of people make cream cheese stuff, and then glop it all up with sweet fruit sauces. In this one, the cheese stands alone.

6 Tb unsalted butter, melted	1 tsp pure vanilla
¼ tsp powdered ginger	⅓ cup sugar
½ tsp cinnamon	2 eggs
1¼ cups graham cracker crumbs	1½ cups sour cream
12 oz. natural cream cheese	1 Tb sugar

Step 1: Make the crust

Mix together butter, ginger, cinnamon and crumbs, using a fork. Turn into a 9-inch pie pan. Press evenly and firmly on bottom and up the sides. Chill.

Step 2: Make the filling, and bake

Mix together the cream cheese, vanilla, ⅓ cup sugar, and eggs. Pour into chilled crust, and bake for exactly 25 minutes at 350 degrees. Remove from oven, and let stand at room temperature for 25 minutes.

Step 3: Make the topping

Combine sour cream and 1 tablespoon sugar. Spread on top, and bake at 300 degrees for 5 minutes. Refrigerate for at least 4 hours before serving.

CHEESE TORTA

Serves 6 to 8

Torta is the Italian word for torte, which is the French word for a cake or pastry prepared with little or no flour. This one is like a light cheesecake—light even though it has a lot of cream cheese in it. It almost seems a little fragile. It's not the dense kind that gets stuck in your throat.

Regarding natural cream cheese: you should be able to find it in many markets and health food stores. You can use supermarket cream cheese (the stuff fortified with vegetable gum) if you must, but in the restaurant, we don't. Natural cream cheese is much fluffier, and always fresher because it doesn't keep forever.

16 oz. natural cream cheese	¾ tsp lemon juice
4 egg yolks	1 tsp lemon rind, grated
⅔ cup sugar	¾ tsp pure vanilla extract
4 tsp flour	4 egg whites
⅔ cup plain yogurt	pinch salt

Beat together cream cheese and egg yolks. Add the sugar, flour, yogurt, lemon juice, lemon rind, and vanilla.

Beat the egg whites with the salt until they form stiff peaks. Fold gently into the cheese mixture. Pour into a greased 9-inch springform pan. Bake at 325 degrees for 1¼ hours. It will jiggle when removed from the oven, and it will deflate, which is all right. (Don't worry if the appearance is not perfect; it will crack a little, which is part of the charm.)

Let cool for 1 hour, release springform collar, and refrigerate for at least 5 hours.

Serve with fresh fruit (grapes on the side, or sliced strawberries or a fruit compote), or with this blueberry sauce:

BLUEBERRY SAUCE

1 lb. fresh or frozen blueberries	¼ cup crème de cassis
1 Tb sugar	3 Tb water

Place all ingredients in a saucepan and bring to a boil over medium heat, stirring occasionally. Boil for 7 to 10 minutes, until mixture has thickened slightly. Mash as few or as many of the berries as you wish. Cool and use for cheesecake, waffles, ice cream, whatever.

RICE PUDDING

Rice pudding is a much maligned dish. It's had bad press. All those little lunch rooms that serve gluey rice pudding in little thick bowls. You know, whenever I make rice pudding at the restaurant, the only people who eat it are the staff. I've never understood that. I guess people have had a lot of bad rice pudding in their lives. I wish they'd trust me. I would never serve gluey rice pudding. In fact, I could live on rice pudding and fried polenta the rest of my life.

This is the same rice pudding I've been making since I was twelve years old. The one difference is that I used to use white sugar, now I use brown, which gives a fuller flavor. Also, I've been using brown rice, which gives it a whole different personality.

5 eggs
3¼ cups milk
½ cup brown sugar
pinch salt
½ tsp cinnamon

¼ tsp nutmeg
½ cup raisins
1 cup cooked rice (white or brown), cooled

Whisk together eggs, milk, brown sugar, salt, cinnamon, and nutmeg. Add rice and raisins, and pour into buttered 8-inch square pan. Set into a 9 × 13 × 2-inch pan filled with water. Bake at 350 degrees for 1 hour. Serve warm or cold, with whipped cream if you wish.

BREAD AND BUTTER PUDDING

This is yet another homey dessert which I am helping to regain its stature. Originally it was invented to use up leftovers. At the restaurant, we make it with stale baguettes, but you can use cookies, cake, biscuits, whatever. You make a very rich custard, throw some raisins in, and cook it carefully in a bain-marie, which is a larger pan filled with water, sort of like a make-shift double boiler.

Our staff goes wild for this dessert. I mean, they would step on each other's toes to get this. I have to remind them to leave some for the customers—"you know, those nice people who make it possible for you to be here."

enough very thinly sliced bread (no more than ¼ inch thick), cake, or brioche to line the bottom of 8 × 8-inch pan

½ cup chocolate chips (or ¼ cup raisins soaked in 2 Tb rum or brandy for 1 hour or more)

2 Tb unsalted butter

3 eggs

2 egg yolks

½ cup brown sugar

pinch salt

1¼ cups milk

1½ cups heavy cream

1½ tsp pure vanilla extract

⅛ tsp nutmeg

⅛ tsp cinnamon

whipped cream (optional)

If using chocolate chips, sprinkle them on the bottom of an unbuttered 8 × 8-inch pan. If using raisins, strain and sprinkle them on the bottom of an 8 × 8-inch pan.

Butter the bread (or whatever you are using) and place it on the layer of chips or raisins. Do not (repeat: *do not*) crowd the bread. It should not be wedged in. You should be able to see between the bread pieces.

Mix together the eggs, egg yolks, sugar, salt, milk and heavy cream, vanilla, nutmeg, and cinnamon. Pour through a strainer into the pan.

Push floating bread slices down into egg mixture. Set pan into a 9 × 13 × 2-inch pan filled partially with hot water. To do this in the most simple manner, put the smaller pan in the larger one and place both in the oven. Bring the hot water over to the pans, thereby avoiding the otherwise inevitable "hot water on the toes" syndrome.

Bake at 325 degrees for 55 minutes. Do *not* let the temperature go above this, or the custard will separate.

Cool pudding at least 1 hour, and serve with whipped cream. (If you have some fresh raspberries, you might break them out at this point, too.)

CHOCOLATE TRUFFLES

I made up this recipe when there was a great to-do over truffles a few years ago. There were recipes all over the place, and I tried most of them. But I guess I was looking for something a little bit different. They were never bitter enough for me. This one is a real chocolate-lover's recipe.

At first, people thought they tasted salty, even though there is no salt in them. Bitter chocolate must have that effect on the tongue; so I added powdered sugar which counteracts that. These truffles are easy and fun to make, and impressive when you're done. I've made them with kids. And they freeze well (the truffles, not the kids).

They are great for desserts or snacks, and they make lovely gifts for people.

1 Tb instant coffee, dissolved in ¼ cup water
8 oz. semisweet chocolate
1 oz. bitter chocolate
3 egg yolks

½ cup unsalted butter, cut into tea-spoon-sized pieces
¼ cup Myer's rum or Grand Marnier
½ cup unsweetened cocoa
¼ cup powdered sugar

Place coffee and both chocolates in the top of a double boiler, and stir with a whisk over medium heat until chocolate has melted. In a separate bowl, beat the egg yolks and add ½ cup of the chocolate mixture to them. Beat well and add back to the chocolate in the pan. Beat well for 2 minutes, cool 5 minutes, then gradually beat in the butter, one piece at a time. Be sure *no* butter is visible, then add the rum or Grand Marnier.

Refrigerate about 1½ hours, until firm enough to form truffles. Use either a pastry tube with a #7 point, or drop from a teaspoon onto a cookie sheet. Just make blobs on the cookie sheet—don't worry about appearance at this point. Re-refrigerate for at least half an hour.

Remove truffles from refrigerator. Combine cocoa and powdered sugar, and place in a container with a lid. Drop truffles into the cocoa mix and shake to coat them. Quickly roll into balls with your hands; the truffles can be irregular in shape. Store in a tightly covered container. Store in refrigerator.

HILDE BURTON'S CHOCOLATE MOUSSE

This isn't involved the way chocolate mousse recipes frequently are. It's simply delicious. I've eaten tons of this mousse, made either by me, or by its creator, Hilde Burton.

When you make this mousse with unsweetened chocolate, the result is a deep, rich, intense chocolate flavor. Semisweet chocolate gives a lighter and, not surprisingly, sweeter flavor. You can always combine two chocolates, too.

MOUSSE

4 eggs, separated

4 oz. semisweet or unsweetened chocolate, melted and cooled

½ cup heavy cream

½ cup powdered sugar

TOPPING

1½ cup heavy cream

2 Tb powdered sugar

2 Tb Grand Marnier

cocoa to sprinkle

In a blender, place the egg yolks, chocolate, ½ cup of the heavy cream, and ½ cup of powdered sugar. Whirl for 2 minutes at the slowest speed.

Add the egg whites, and blend for another 3 minutes. The mixture will be quite light. Pour mixture into a serving bowl, or individual glasses, and place in the refrigerator for at least 4 hours.

At serving time, whip 1½ cups heavy cream with 2 tablespoons powdered sugar and Grand Marnier until soft peaks form. Divide among each serving, and sprinkle the whipped cream with cocoa.

CRÈME FRAÎCHE

This is one of our basic pantry items. All it is is soured cream. In France, dairy products are different from those we get in America, with regard to amounts of bacteria growth and homogenization. The French can buy crème fraîche; we have to make it. But *do* because it has so many uses. Straight, on fruit. Whipped, in soups. Stirred into sauces. The thing that's so wonderful about it is that it doesn't break down when it's heated the way sour cream or yogurt does. It also has a mellower flavor—sort of nutty, instead of tangy. I love it, and use it in place of sour cream all the time.

You can whip it and make it thicker, the same way you do whipping cream, or you can use it in the more liquid stage.

heavy cream (as many cups as you wish)

buttermilk (1 Tb for each cup of heavy cream)

Combine heavy cream and buttermilk in a saucepan over medium heat. Heat just until the chill is off—to about 90 degrees. Pour into a glass jar, cover lightly with a piece of waxed paper, and let sit in a warm place (65 to 70 degrees) for 12 to 20 hours, until the crème fraîche has thickened.

Replace waxed paper with plastic wrap or a tight-fitting lid, and refrigerate for at least 6 hours before using. Keeps up to 2 weeks.

CHOCOLATE CRÈME FRAÎCHE FROSTING

*Enough for a
9-inch cake*

This is adapted from a chocolate frosting recipe made with sour cream. I am not a fan of sour cream in situations where the tanginess seems inappropriate. That's why I don't like chocolate cheesecake, for instance. So one day, it occurred to me to make chocolate frosting with crème fraîche. It supplies the necessary thickness without the tang. It's very easy to make. The chocolate must be warm, to slightly cook the egg yolks. So once you make the frosting, you must frost the cake within 10 minutes.

This is especially good with the Amazon Chocolate Cake (see page 210) and the Chocolate Sour Cream Fudge Cake (see page 212).

1 cup Crème Fraîche (see page 244)   1 lb. semisweet chocolate, melted
2 egg yolks   and kept warm

With an electric mixer, beat together crème fraîche and egg yolks. Add melted chocolate, and beat for 2 minutes or until very thick. Let sit 10 minutes, beat again briefly, and use immediately.

CRÈME PÂTISSIÈRE

Makes 1¼ cups

Crème pâtissière is a thick, rich pastry cream, which you can make in a variety of flavors: chocolate, rum, or coffee, for instance.

Unlike most custards, you can bring this to a boil, and it won't curdle, because it has flour to stabilize it. You can use it as a cake filling, to fill tarts, or to lick from the ends of your fingers.

3 egg yolks
5 Tb sugar
2 Tb + 2 tsp flour
1 cup milk, heated
1 Tb + 2 tsp unsalted butter

1 tsp pure vanilla extract
pinch salt
optional flavorings: 2 oz. unsweetened chocolate, 2 Tb rum, or 3 Tb very strong coffee

Beat egg yolks and sugar together. Add flour and continue to beat until thoroughly blended. Add heated milk and place pan over heat, stirring constantly and thoroughly with a whisk until thickened. The mixture can come to a boil briefly.

Lower heat and cook for 3 minutes, continuing to stir. Remove from heat and stir in butter, vanilla, and salt. Strain. Cool. Add flavorings of choice (chocolate, rum, coffee) or use as is.

MOCHA BUTTERCREAM

Enough to frost a 9-inch cake, or the Amazon Chocolate Cake on page 210

There are two kinds of buttercream: cooked and uncooked. The cooked type, involving hot sugar syrup, is often thought to be better than that creamed butter and sugar type we all grew up with as frosting. This is an uncooked version that tastes just as good as the more complicated cooked ones.

This is superb on the Amazon Chocolate Cake (see page 210), or indeed on any other cake. I've never had the nerve to serve a bowl of frosting as a free-standing dessert, but it could work with this one. Mocha is a rather complex taste.

2 oz. bitter chocolate, melted and cooled
1 Tb instant coffee
2 Tb espresso

1 cup unsalted butter, softened
2 cups powdered sugar, sifted
1 egg yolk

In the top of a double boiler, place bitter chocolate, instant coffee, and espresso and stir over medium heat until melted. Let cool slightly. Place butter, sugar and egg yolk in bowl of a food processor fitted with a steel S-blade. Blend thoroughly, and add chocolate and coffee-espresso mix. Blend and chill to spreading consistency—about 15 minutes.

VANILLA CUSTARD SAUCE

This is what's called a pouring custard, or *crème anglaise*. You can serve it with a soufflé, or with a chocolate cake—either pouring the sauce over the top, or, as the fashion seems to be these days, pouring the sauce onto the plate and putting the dessert on top of the sauce. You can change the flavor of this sauce with such simple additions as: 1 tablespoon of rum, and 1 tablespoon of instant coffee dissolved in 1½ teaspoons of water; or 2 ounces of melted chocolate (bitter or semisweet), etc.

Egg-based preparations like this sometimes curdle, no matter how careful you are. If this happens, the really simple solution is to let the mixture cool for 15 minutes, and whirl briefly in a blender and strain. This always works perfectly.

I've been getting fantastic vanilla beans from Tahiti. They're not the dried out skinny things we're used to; they are obese. They are moist, and perfumy and twice the size of ordinary beans, at about the same price. If we can get a steady and reliable supply, we hope to offer them by mail (see page 256).

2 cups milk	⅓ cup sugar
½ vanilla bean, split down the center	pinch salt
6 egg yolks	½ tsp pure vanilla extract

In a heavy saucepan, place the milk and vanilla bean. Scald, then set aside.

Place egg yolks, sugar, and salt in a bowl and whisk vigorously until light. Add the scalded milk and vanilla bean, stirring, and pour back into the saucepan.

Cook over moderate heat, stirring until it thickens, *but do not let it boil*. Remove from heat and stir in vanilla extract. Strain custard, then scrape inside of vanilla bean pod into custard. Cool, stirring occasionally, and chill covered.

Note: If the mixture curdles, let cool for 15 minutes, then whirl briefly in a blender and strain. Works every time.

FUDGE SAUCE

Makes about 2½ cups

The perfect fudge sauce is the least adulterated. I encounter a lot of sauce recipes with corn syrup, and I can't figure out why it's in there. If you have a good chocolate, you don't need anything else, except the half and half to thin it down a little. I use Ghirardelli bittersweet chocolate, which can be found in most stores. You can refrigerate this sauce, then warm it up later in a double boiler.

1 lb. semisweet chocolate, in small   1 cup half and half
    chunks

In the top of a double boiler, place both ingredients. Melt over simmering water, whisk together, and pour over ice cream.

Index

Mail Order Information

We're talking about two kinds of mail order products here: those splendid confections that we make ourselves in the Cafe Beaujolais Bakery, and those items made by our friends, neighbors, and suppliers, which we also sell by mail.

As tempting as it was to give detailed ordering information right here in the book, there are two good reasons why I chose not to do so—prices change, and items change, too. For instance, I plan to expand our own product line, and to add new suppliers from time to time, either to supplement or replace those we use now. So what makes the most sense is to ask you to write (or call) for our current mail order literature. We will send it to you promptly, with order forms and complete instructions.

For complete information, please write or call:

Cafe Beaujolais Bakery
P.O. Box 730-B
Mendocino, California 95460
(707) 964-0294

Among the products available by mail are these:

Our own:
Panforte di Mendocino: an Italian-style nut confection 22-ounce wheels, in almond, walnut, hazelnut or macadamia nut.

Original Dried Fruit Fruitcake: a 20-ounce cake.

Chocolate Dried Fruit Fruitcake: also a 20-ounce wonder.

Our friends:
Grand Finale Buttercream Caramels and Dessert Sauces: very special candy, available in various flavors (including mocha, chocolate, and bourbon pecan); and dessert sauces (including triple chocolate fudge, and white chocolate with raspberry liqueur essence).

Fuller's Fine Herbs. Artful blends of locally grown herbs. The one called Beaujolais Blend is mentioned frequently throughout this book, and used regularly at Cafe Beaujolais.